BIG BOOK
OF BOOKS
AND ACTIVITIES

dma
dinah-might adventures, LP

Copyright ©1992, Dinah Zike
Dinah-Might Adventures, LP
P.O. Box 690328
San Antonio, Texas 78269-0328 USA
Office: (210) 698-0123
Fax: (210) 698-0095
Orders only: 1-800-99-DINAH (993-4624)
Catalog/Orders e-mail: orders@dinah.com
Workshop E-mail: dma@dinah.com
Website: www.dinah.com

Dinah Zike's

BIG BOOK
OF BOOKS
AND ACTIVITIES

An illustrated guide for teachers, parents,
and anyone who works with kids!

by Dinah Zike, M.Ed.

EDITOR
Suzanne Powers
ARTIST
Jessie Flores
PHOTOGRAPHY, LAYOUT, AND BOOK DESIGN
Ignacio Salas-Humara

Other Books and Videos by Dinah Zike

BIG BOOK OF BOOKS AND ACTIVITIES
BIG BOOK OF PROJECTS
BIG BOOK OF MATH GRAPHICS
BIG BOOK OF HOLIDAY ACTIVITIES
GREAT TABLES, GRAPHS, CHARTS, DIAGRAMS, ETC. YOU CAN MAKE!
SCIENCE POEMS, RIDDLES, RHYMES---SPACE
THE EARTH SCIENCE BOOK
VIDEO: HOW TO USE THE BIG BOOK OF BOOKS
VIDEO: HOW TO USE THE BIG BOOK OF PROJECTS
TIME TWISTERS: THE LOST NAVIGATORS
TIME TWISTERS: THE HIDDEN CAVERNS
TIME TWISTERS: RAIN FOREST RESCUE
TIME TWISTERS: THE SEARCH FOR T. REX
THE WORLD OF PLANTS
THE WORLD OF TOOLS AND TECHNOLOGY
THE WORLD OF SPACE
THE WORLD OF INSECTS AND ARACHNIDS

This book is dedicated...

...to my parents, Coney and Catherine Dorough, who always allowed me the freedom to be creative.

...to the teachers, parents, and students in universities, school districts, and homes across the world who have helped me design, develop, and adapt the manipulatives and activities presented in this book.

A special thank you to...

...Cecile Richards who has been such an asset to Dinah-Might Activities through the years, and to her husband Sonny who prints books faster than we can produce them.

...Charles Steinman who can be called at two a.m. for help!

...Ballinger I.S.D., Ballinger, Texas for allowing us to share photographs taken during our visit in March, 1992.

...all the students and teachers whose work and ideas are included in this book.

...all the people who have waited so patiently for us to get this book finished!

An extra-special thank you to...

...Greystoke, Growl Tiger, and Mango for their patience, love, and understanding.

Table of Contents

Dear Parent,

Children are bombarded with words during their formative years (birth to twelve years), but it is the words that are demonstrated through actions that form the child.

So much of what you teach your child is done through demonstration. You demonstrate how to act and how to talk. You show through your actions what is right and wrong. Your attitude toward learning is also demonstrated by your involvement or lack of involvement in your child's mental and creative growth and development.

When parents ask me, "What can I do to help my child in school?" my response is always the same. It is vitally important that the home be established as a positive environment for learning. The prevailing attitude in the home must be one that places a great importance on exploring, questioning, investigating, and discovering.

One of the ways in which I encourage parents to create a learning, exploring, creating environment is illustrated in this book. A house that is filled with inexpensive materials used to make books and projects that encourage the child to read, write, reason, research, and discover the world, is an environment that shouts the importance of learning.

Spend time with your child making the projects in this book. Supplement classroom work with exciting activities at home. Encourage your child to use these projects to enhance required school work and science fair projects. Replace some of the time spent on coloring books, comic books, television shows, and computer games with creative learning activities.

Read to your child. Write to your child. Share stories and experiences. Explore the world together. I hope that this book will provide another opportunity to meaningfully demonstrate within your home the joy of learning creatively.

For the Love of Learning,

Dinah Zike

Dear Educator,

The world of education is continually in a state of change. You will experience many trendy teaching styles that will be in vogue just long enough for you to buy all of the new activity booklets and get the supplemental aids necessary to teach the program properly. Then about the time you are getting comfortable with the new curriculum, it goes out of style! You must make way for the new "salvation for education" or you will be viewed as a poor teacher and an obstacle to change.

If you teach long enough, you will live to see this old program resurface. The teaching techniques and the philosophy of this new program will be the same as the one you experienced in the past, only the catchy terms and the program's name have changed!

Yet, through the years there have been certain elements of continuity that never vanish - paper, pencils, scissors, and glue have always been available on elementary campuses. As I travel around the country working with teachers, parents, and students, these basic materials - combined with literature, newspapers and magazines, maps and globes, and physical objects I collect - become my basic teaching aids.

These simple materials that teachers have used with students for centuries can be transformed into wonderful learning aids and manipulatives that seem more like craft projects than learning experiences. The manipulatives are "made for the moment." They are not made to be laminated and stored after use, but to be shared with everyone within the child's world.

Instead of fill-in-the-blank activities, use paper and pencils to make action learning aids that incorporate reading and writing, math and science, map and globe skills, and critical thinking. However, the main advantages of this use of pencil, paper, scissors, and glue is that it stimulates creativity while teaching students responsibility for their own learning process.

These teaching aids are timeless. No matter what your teaching style - whole language, cooperative learning, thematic units, multidisciplinary integration, etc. - you will be able to use these basic folds and ideas to create your own exciting and challenging student oriented activities.

Learning is a lifetime job and a lifetime joy! I hope you have as much fun and success sharing these activities with your students as I have had in designing them for mine.

For the Love of Learning,

Dinah Zike

ESTABLISHING AN ENVIRONMENT FOR CREATIVITY

You can help children be creative by placing them in an environment that encourages creativity. It is important for children to have easy access to paper, pencils, crayons, markers, and other supplies. This encourages expression through writing, designing, illustrating, and building.

Set up a "publishing center" or "creative center" in your classroom or home. Fill it with scratch paper, paper scraps, brightly colored paper, clean white paper, lined paper, and other supplies. Below, you will find some hints on how to get started.

SCRATCH PAPER

Any business with a copy machine has scratch paper. Copy machines seem to produce an excess of unwanted, unusable paper. Get permission to place a brightly colored box beside a copy machine with a sign that reads "Scratch Paper Needed." People are happy to recycle this paper, and you will obtain ample paper for your school or home creative center.

SCRAP PAPER

Keep a brightly colored box labeled "Paper Scraps" in your publishing center. Fragments of paper left over from cutting and hole punching can be converted into illustrations and decorations on projects, reports, and creative writing booklets.

PURCHASED PAPER

Make only small quantities of paper available at a time. Store excess paper, restocking as needed.

Brightly Colored Paper (8 1/2" x 11") - Buy whole reams of colored paper (500 sheets) at any office supply store. Each piece of paper will cost less than two cents a sheet.

White Copy Paper (8 1/2" x 11") - Can be purchased by the ream or the case (10 reams).

White Copy Paper (11" x 17") - This is the largest copy paper available, and it can be used to make large books and projects for young children. Make "lap books" that you read to your child, or use this paper with older students for class reports and special activities.

Construction Paper (9" x 12") - Is larger than copy paper; therefore, it makes great covers for books made out of 8 1/2" x 11" copy paper.

Notebook Paper - Lined notebook paper can be cut into sections to fit inside books or projects, or used as whole sheets.

WRITING PAPER AND HOMEMADE STATIONERY

Use small pieces of paper and quick writing activities to increase a child's writing skills and confidence. These small pieces of paper can be glued into the books and projects presented in this book. Often a child uses only a small portion of a standard piece of paper for an illustration, wasting the rest of the sheet. Use small pieces of paper for illustrations. Keep narrow strips of paper for recording new words or interesting sentences.

Cut sheets of paper in fourths and have them available in your publishing or creative center for asking questions, making complaints, recording facts, labeling objects, writing notes, etc. Half sheets should also be available for longer writing activities or for larger illustrations.

Use both of these paper sizes with the sentence strip holder illustrated in this book.

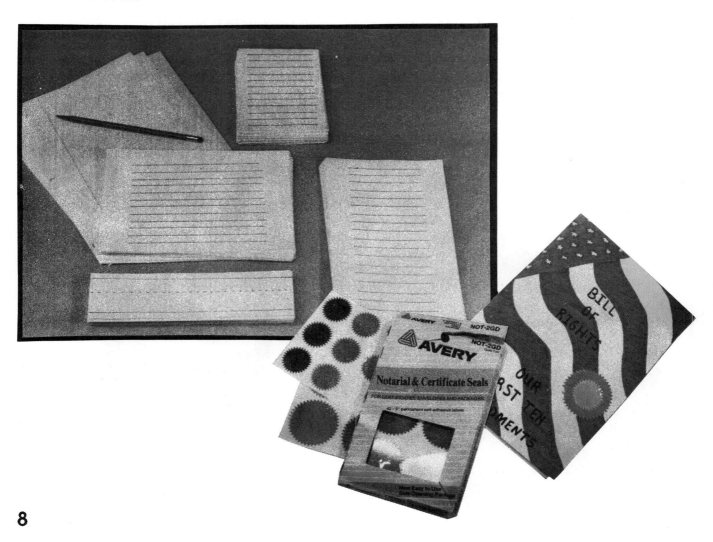

SUPPLIES NEEDED

-good scissors
-a box of crayons
-a set of water based markers for coloring
-a permanent marker for labeling
-colored pencils
-liquid glue — *Elmer's Blue Gel is better than white*
-stapler and staples
-12" ruler
-hole punch
-food coloring/cake icing dye
-zip-lock bags
-spray adhesive* — *the Best 3M Brand only*
-rubbing alcohol**

ODDS AND ENDS

-pieces of ribbon or yarn
-pieces of aluminum foil
-pieces of wax paper
-stickers
-magazine pictures
-stamps and stamp pads
-buttons
-notebook rings
-envelopes

*   Spray adhesives should be used by adults only. Pictures, student work, posters, charts, and other paper projects are secured smoothly without glue marks when a spray is used.

**   Used to dye macaroni and cornmeal. To be used under the supervision of an adult helper.

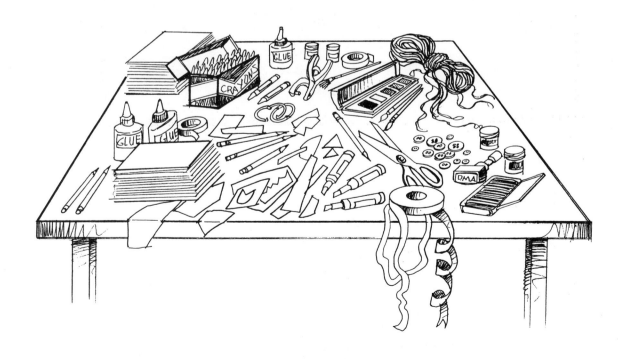

STORAGE - BOOK BAGS

One-gallon zip-lock bags are ideal for storing ongoing projects and books students are writing and researching.

Use a strip of clear, 2" tape to secure 1" x 1" pieces of index card to the top corner of a bag, front and back. Punch a hole through the index cards and the bag. Use a giant notebook ring to keep several of the "Book Bags" together.

Label the bags by writing on them with a permanent marker.

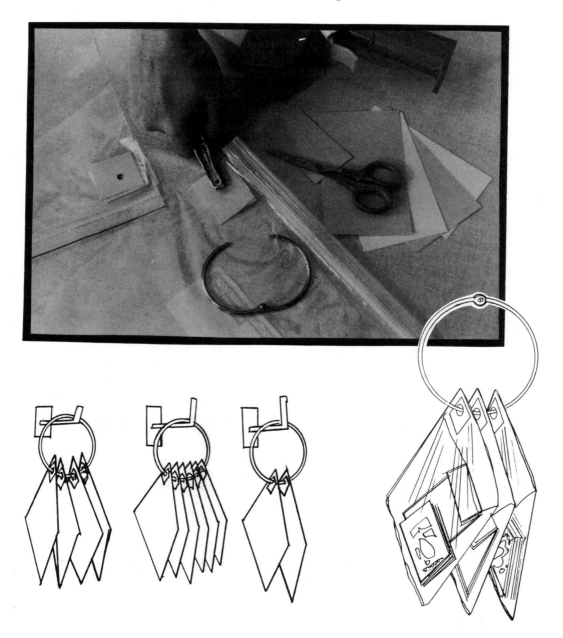

PHOTO SECTION

Everyone needs to feel important. A positive self identity is valuable to children and adults alike.

Take black and white photographs of your child or students in your classroom. It is possible to photograph 2 children at a time, getting a good close-up shot of both of their faces. Cut the developed pictures apart. Tape all of the small photographs on an 8 1/2" x 11" sheet of paper and make numerous photocopies.

Cut the pictures apart and store them in the publishing center for easy access. As students write a book or design a project, have them write an "About the Author" or "About the Illustrator" section and include a photograph with it.

A simple photo storage container is illustrated below.

Glue small jewelry boxes to a cardboard case.

GLUE HINTS

Many of the folds and projects illustrated in this book can be made into larger, more lengthy books or projects by gluing individual folded sections together, "side-by-side."

Remember to use small amounts of glue except when noted. Always place glue 1/4" from the edge of the paper so it does not ooze out around the edges of the object being glued.

When gluing large projects, place a small amount of glue in a tiny cap or lid, and use cotton tips to spread the glue on the paper. *(Classroom Organization: It Can Be Done, Dinah Zike, 1989.)*

AVOIDING FRUSTRATION AND FAILURE WHEN MAKING BOOKS IN THE ELEMENTARY CLASSROOM

1. Introduce the steps for a new project at least one week before you plan to use them in a lesson. Use scratch paper to make the book the first time.

2. If five students understand the process after the first fast demonstration, you have been successful.

3. During the week, students can practice making the book using scratch paper. Some students might want to take scratch paper home to make books.

4. When half of the class knows how to make the book, you are ready to incorporate it into a lesson. Place the students "one-on-one." A student who knows how to make a book can help a student who does not.

NAMES OF FOLDS AND OTHER TERMS

Every fold has two parts. The outside edge formed by a fold is called the "mountain." The inside of this edge is the "valley."

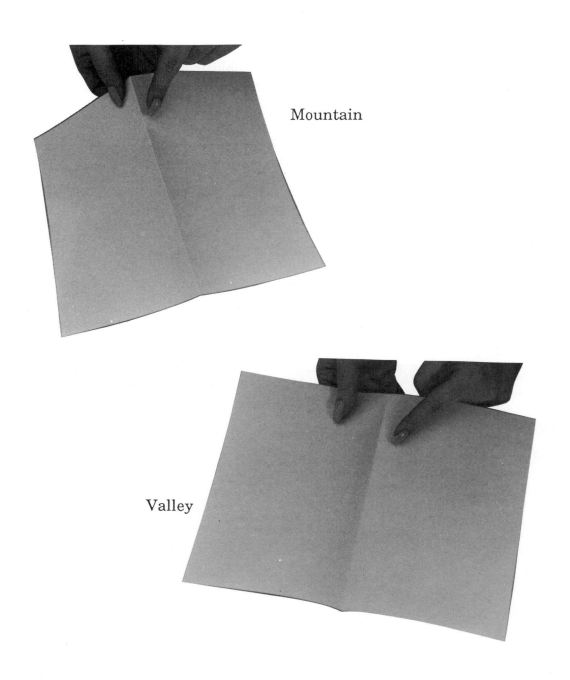

Mountain

Valley

NAMES OF FOLDS AND OTHER TERMS

These basic folds will be used throughout this book.   Their unusual names will help you remember the shape of the fold.

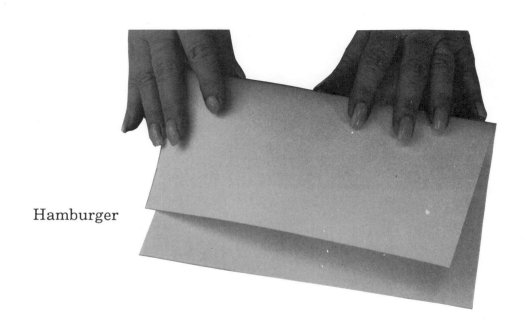

Hamburger

NAMES OF FOLDS AND OTHER TERMS

Hot Dog

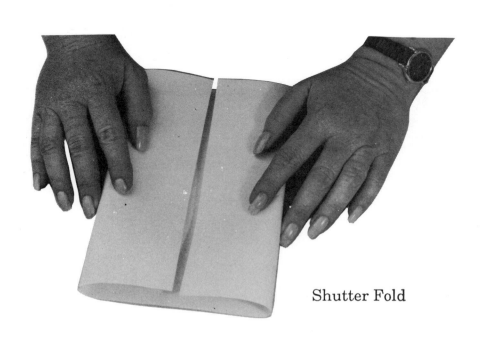

Shutter Fold

NAMES OF FOLDS AND OTHER TERMS

Burrito

Taco

HALF-BOOKS

Fold a sheet of paper (8 1/2" x 11") in half. This book can be made vertically (hot dog) or horizontally (hamburger). If made like a hamburger it can be placed on a sentence strip holder with the "book title" on the front and "about the author" on the back.

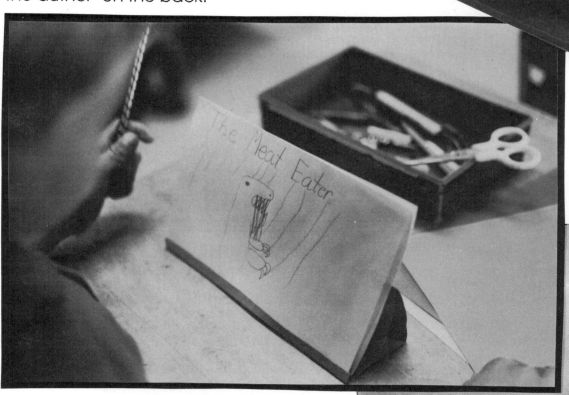

FOLDED BOOKS

Begin with a Half Book. Fold it in half like a hamburger. This makes a ready-made cover and a two page spread for information on the inside. This book can also be made out of a work sheet to take advantage of the blank side of paper.

LARGE QUESTION
AND ANSWER BOOK

Take a Folded Book and cut up the valley of the inside fold toward the mountain top. This cut forms two large tabs that can be used front and back for writing and illustrations. The book can be expanded by making several of these folds and gluing them side-by-side. Use this book for larger pictures or classroom books.

LARGE VOCABULARY BOOK

Take the Large Question and Answer Book and make an additional cut in the center of each tab toward the mountain top. This will leave four large vocabulary tabs, forming a Large Vocabulary Book.

3/4 BOOKS

Take the Large Question and Answer Book and raise the left hand tab. Cut the tab off at the top fold line. This will leave a quarter sheet of paper that can be placed in a publishing center. More focus can be given to a subject area while using this book by; drawing on the left side, placing questions on the front of the right tab, then listing the answers underneath. An entire unit of study can be covered using 3/4 books. A larger book of information can be made by gluing several 3/4 books side-by-side.

POCKET BOOK

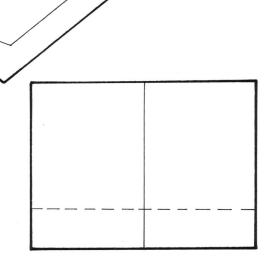

1. Fold a sheet of paper (8 1/2" x 11") in half like a hamburger.

2. Open the folded paper and fold one of the long sides up two inches to form a pocket. Refold along the hamburger fold so that the newly formed pockets are to the inside.

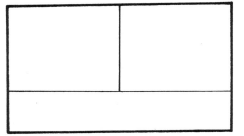

3. Glue the outer edges of the two inch fold with a small amount of glue.

4. Glue a construction paper cover around the pocket book.

variation:

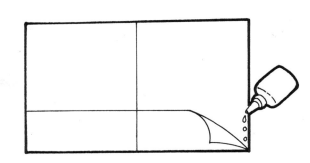

1. Make a multi-paged booklet by gluing several pockets "side-by-side."

2. Glue a construction paper cover around the multi-page pocket booklet.

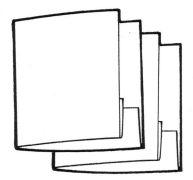

POCKET BOOK

Glue pockets "side-by-side" to
make lengthy pocket books.

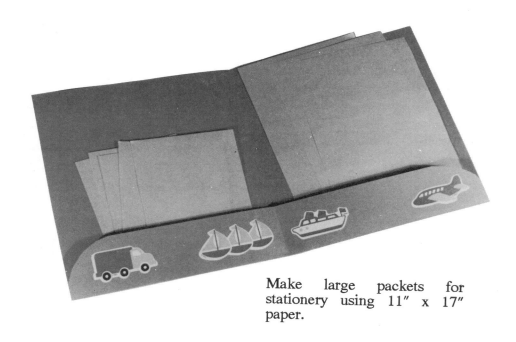

Make large packets for
stationery using 11" x 17"
paper.

24

POCKET BOOK

Collect small pages of notes or illustrations in pocket books. Perfect for library research.

Hot dog fold pocket book.

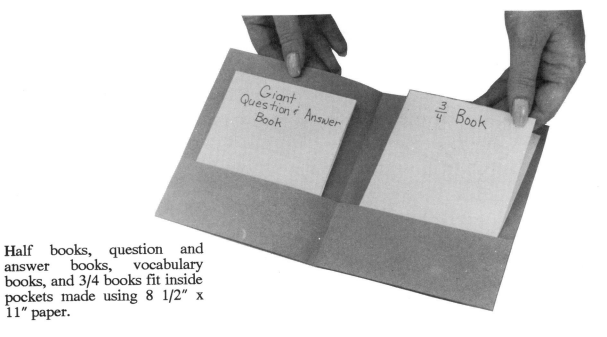

Half books, question and answer books, vocabulary books, and 3/4 books fit inside pockets made using 8 1/2" x 11" paper.

LARGE MATCHBOOK

1. Fold a sheet of paper (8 1/2" x 11") like a hamburger, but fold it so that one side is one inch longer than the other side.

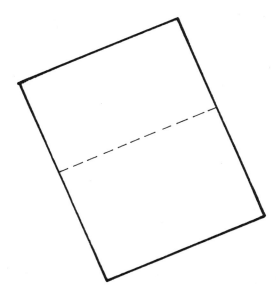

2. Fold the one inch tab over the short side forming an envelope-like fold.

3. Cut the book in half making two large match books.

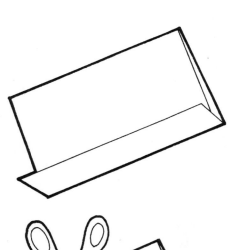

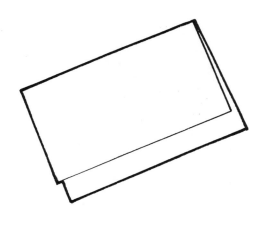

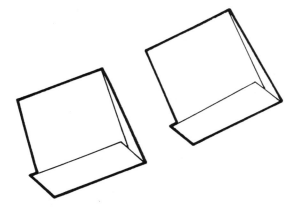

LARGE MATCHBOOK

Use large matchbooks for action bulletin boards. Examples:

Outside	Inside
Question	Answer
Book Title	Synopsis
Character	Description
Setting	Explanation
Math Fact	Answer
Shape of a State	Information
Solar System Planets	Data

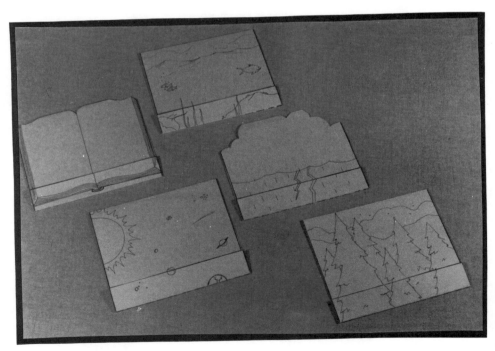

Matchbooks can be made to coordinate with a unit of study or a classroom theme.

LARGE MATCHBOOK

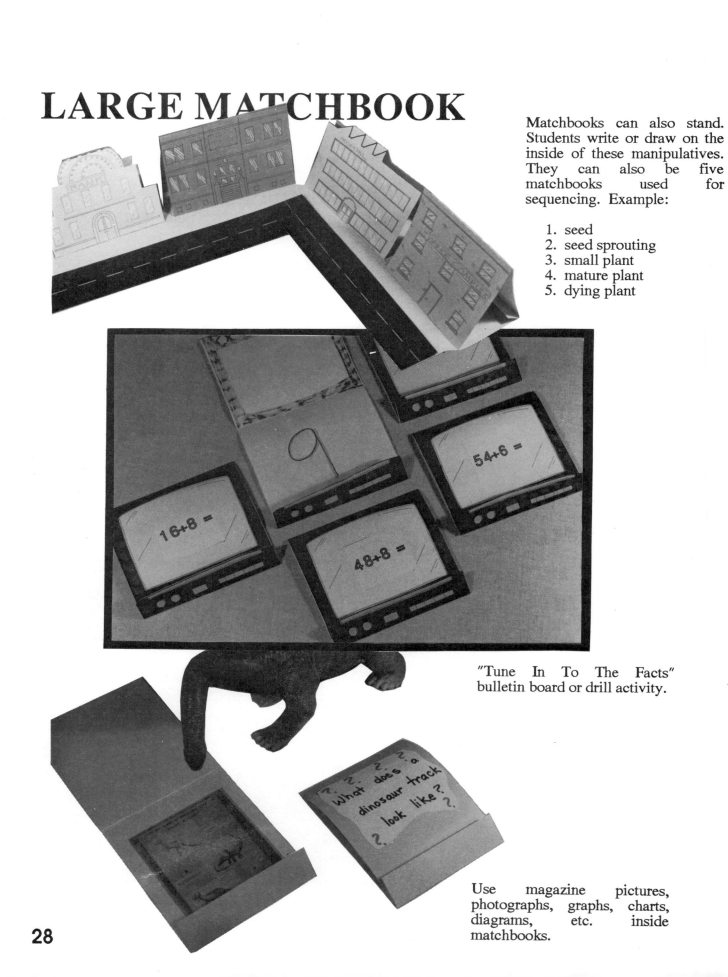

Matchbooks can also stand. Students write or draw on the inside of these manipulatives. They can also be five matchbooks used for sequencing. Example:

1. seed
2. seed sprouting
3. small plant
4. mature plant
5. dying plant

"Tune In To The Facts" bulletin board or drill activity.

Use magazine pictures, photographs, graphs, charts, diagrams, etc. inside matchbooks.

LARGE MATCHBOOK

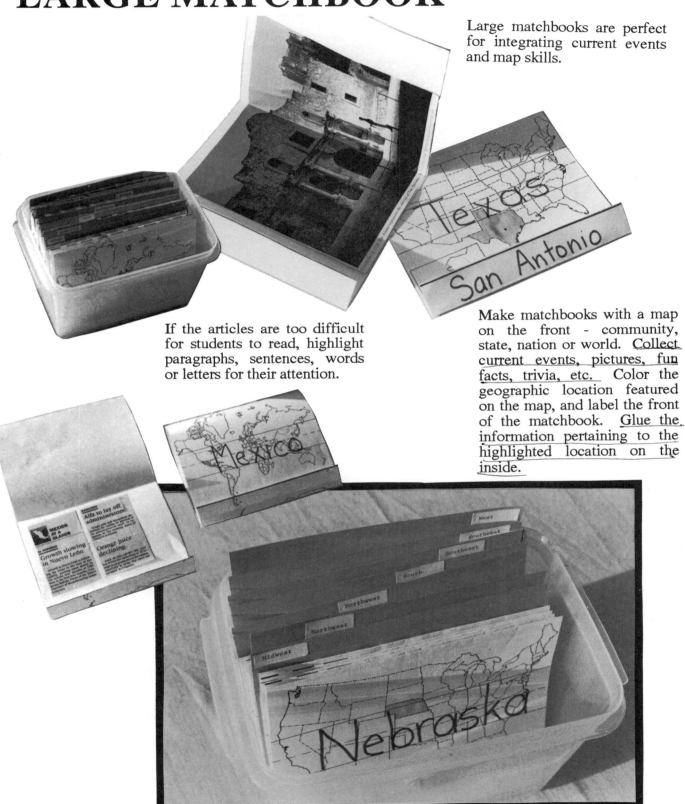

Large matchbooks are perfect for integrating current events and map skills.

If the articles are too difficult for students to read, highlight paragraphs, sentences, words or letters for their attention.

Make matchbooks with a map on the front - community, state, nation or world. Collect current events, pictures, fun facts, trivia, etc. Color the geographic location featured on the map, and label the front of the matchbook. Glue the information pertaining to the highlighted location on the inside.

Make current event files and/or use these matchbooks on bulletin boards.

LARGE MATCHBOOK

Make shaped matchbooks for special projects on bulletin boards.

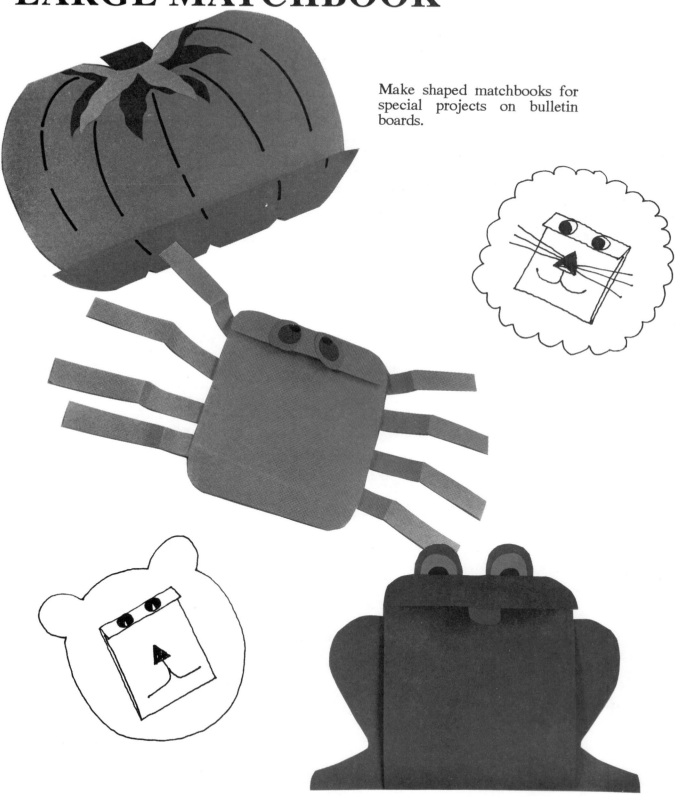

MINIATURE MATCHBOOK

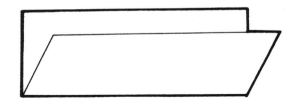

1. Fold a sheet of paper (8 1/2" x 11") in half like a hot dog.

2. Cut the sheet in half along the fold line.

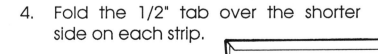

3. Fold the two long strips in half like hot dogs, leaving one side 1/2" shorter than the other side.

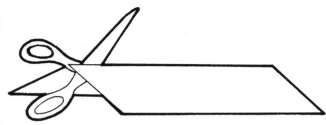

4. Fold the 1/2" tab over the shorter side on each strip.

5. Cut each of the two strips in half forming four halves. Then cut each half into thirds making twelve miniature match books.

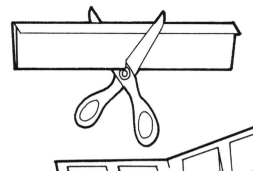

6. Glue the 12 small match books inside a hamburger fold. (3 rows of 4 each)

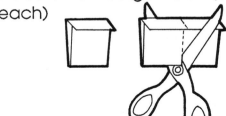
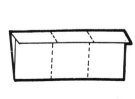

MINIATURE MATCHBOOK

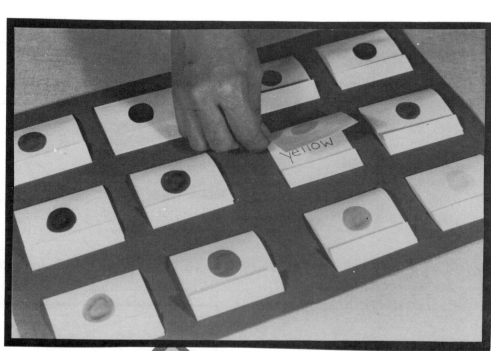

For young children, make matchbooks out of 11" x 17" paper. It will be easier for them to open and close the tabs.

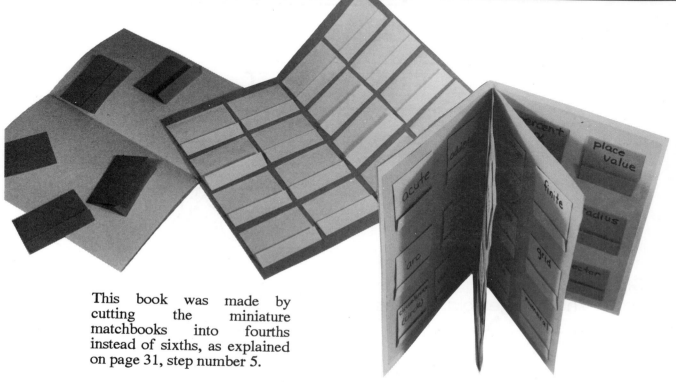

This book was made by cutting the miniature matchbooks into fourths instead of sixths, as explained on page 31, step number 5.

Glue miniature matchbook pages side-by-side to make vocabulary books.

MINIATURE MATCHBOOK

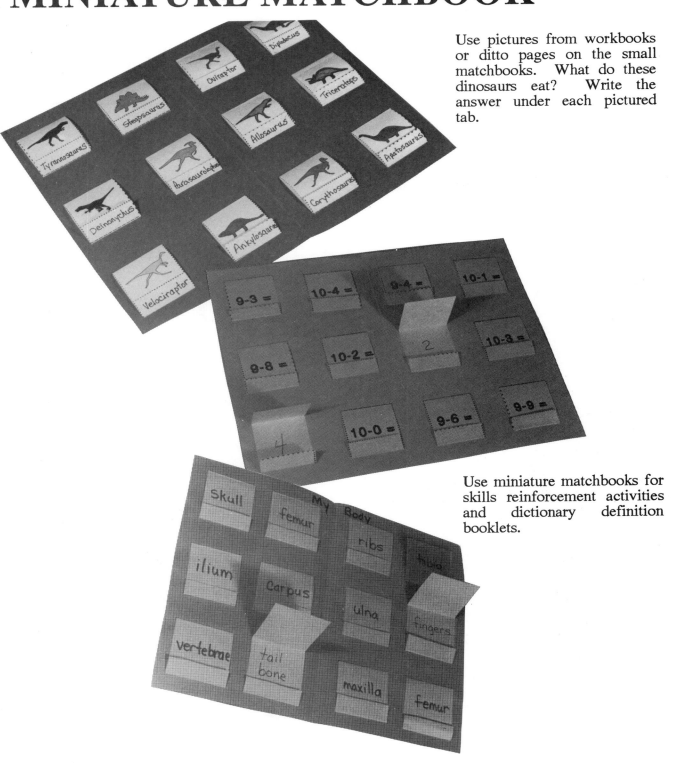

Use pictures from workbooks or ditto pages on the small matchbooks. What do these dinosaurs eat? Write the answer under each pictured tab.

Use miniature matchbooks for skills reinforcement activities and dictionary definition booklets.

MINI BOOK PATTERN

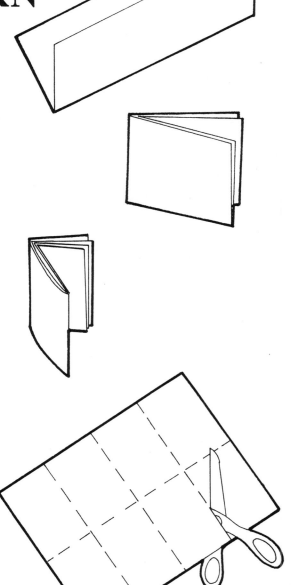

1. Fold a sheet of paper (8 1/2" x 11") in half like a hot dog.

2. Fold it in half again like a hamburger.

3. Then fold in half again forming eights.

4. Open the fold and cut the eight sections apart.

5. Place all eight sections in a stack and fold in half like a hamburger.

6. Staple along the center fold line. Glue the front and back sheets into a construction paper cover.

  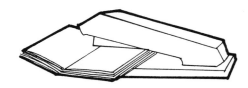

MINI BOOK PATTERN

Make a library of mini books.

Mini books are perfect for stamp collections and sticker books.

MINI BOOK PATTERN

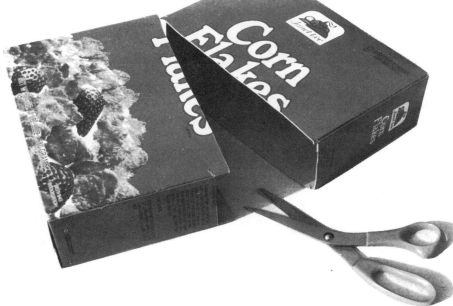

To make your mini book library shelves...

1. Use a cereal box that is at least 3″ wide.

2. Cut the ends off the box to form shelves 2″ deep.

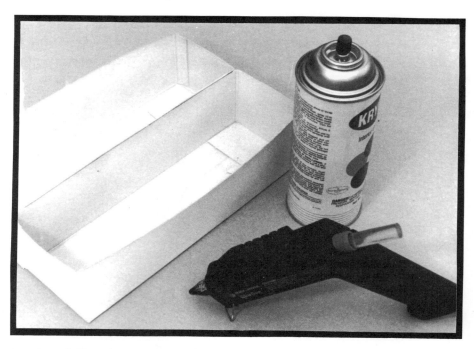

3. Carefully, hot glue the shelves together.

4. Paint the shelves or cover them with contact paper.

CIRCLE STAND

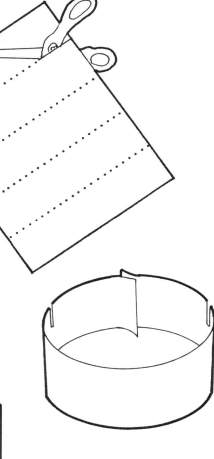

1. Take a fifth sheet of paper and glue the ends together forming a circle.

2. Make a half inch cut on the opposite sides of the circle.

3. Place another fifth sheet with a student's name or an item's identification in the cut openings to create a stand for labeling.

NOTE: Save the paper strips that are cut off when making a taco. They are the perfect size for making a circle stand.

Use circle stands to hold labels, vocabulary words, information cards, and more.

For example, if a student brings something to class to share with others, have them make a circle stand that displays their name and information about the object.

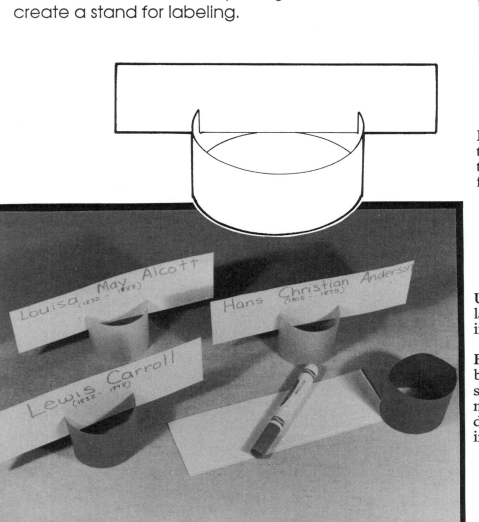

PYRAMID PATTERN

1. Fold a sheet of paper (8 1/2" x 11") into a taco forming a square. Cut off the excess tab formed by the fold.

2. Open the folded taco and refold it the opposite way forming another taco and an X fold pattern.

3. Cut up one of the folds to the center of the X and stop. This forms two triangular shaped flaps.

4. Glue one of the flaps under the other flap forming a pyramid.

PYRAMID PATTERN

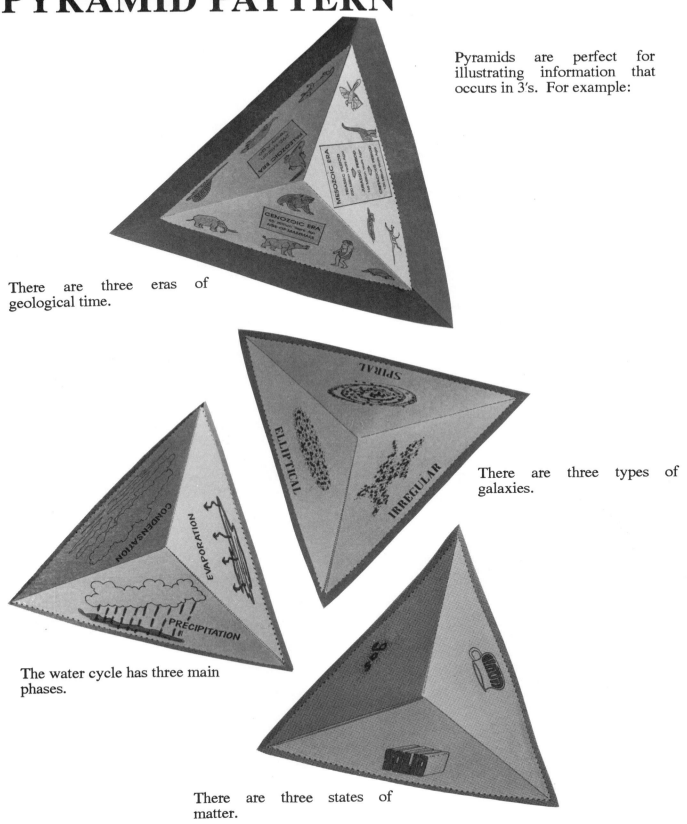

Pyramids are perfect for illustrating information that occurs in 3's. For example:

There are three eras of geological time.

There are three types of galaxies.

The water cycle has three main phases.

There are three states of matter.

PYRAMID PATTERN

Glue four pyramids "side-by-side" to make this diaroma.

Note: Two pyramids glued side-by-side make a nice comparing and contrasting diorama.

40

PYRAMID PATTERN

Use the pyramid patterns to make a mobile. Hang objects from the center of the base of each triangular side.

To hang an object from the middle of the pyramid, connect a string to the knotted string used to hang the mobile.

Several mobiles can be connected to form one long mobile.

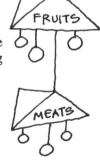

DESK TOP PROJECTS

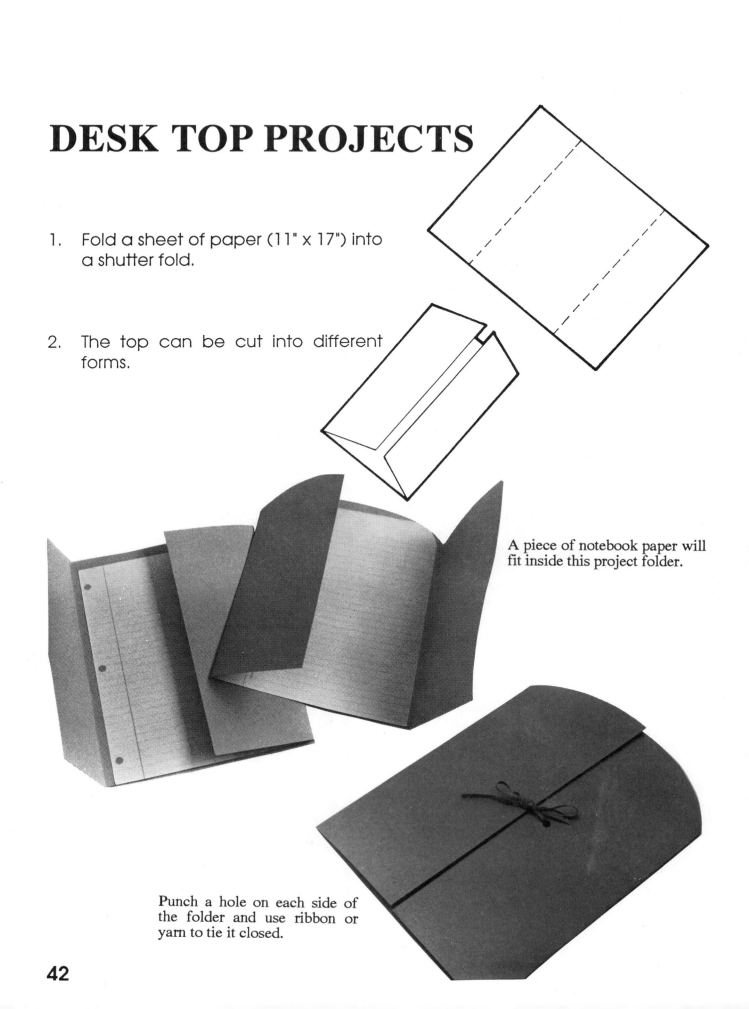

1. Fold a sheet of paper (11" x 17") into a shutter fold.

2. The top can be cut into different forms.

A piece of notebook paper will fit inside this project folder.

Punch a hole on each side of the folder and use ribbon or yarn to tie it closed.

DESK TOP PROJECTS

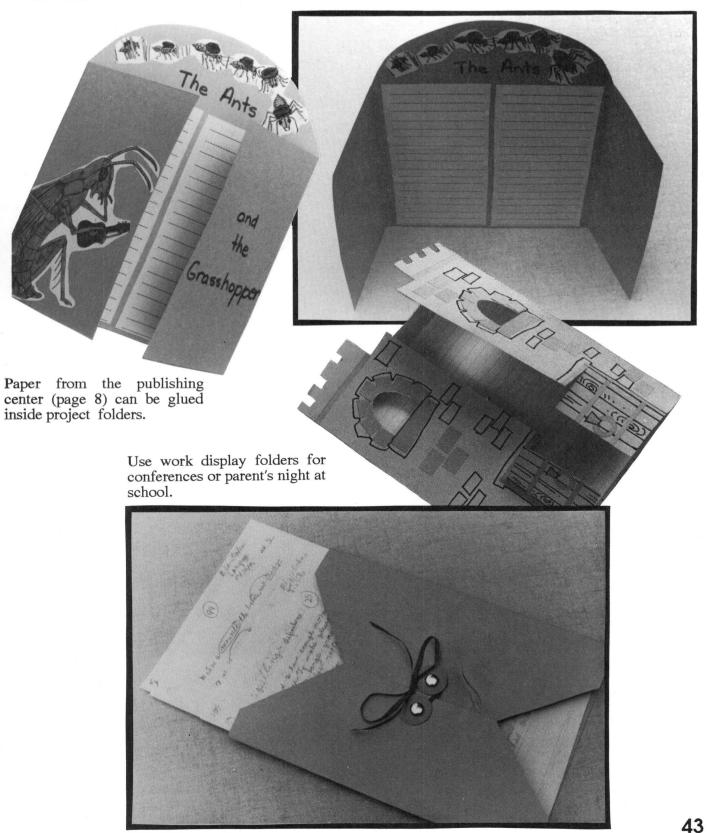

Paper from the publishing center (page 8) can be glued inside project folders.

Use work display folders for conferences or parent's night at school.

SENTENCE STRIP HOLDER

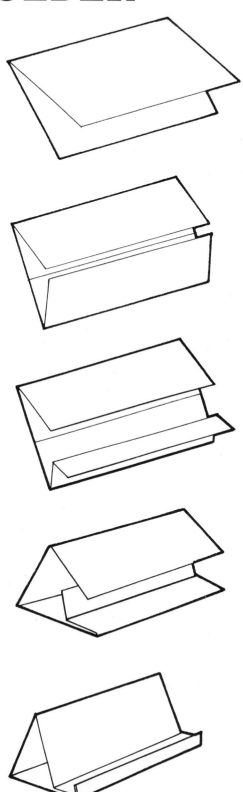

1. Fold a sheet of paper (8 1/2" x 11") in half like a hamburger.

2. Open the hamburger and fold the two outer edges toward the valley. This forms a shutter fold.

3. Fold one of the inside edges of the shutter back to the outside fold. This fold forms a floppy L.

4. Glue the floppy L tab down to the base so that it forms a strong straight L tab.

5. Glue the other shutter side to the front of this L tab. This forms a tent that is the backboard for the flash cards or student work to be displayed.

6. Fold the edge of the L up 1/4" to 1/2" to form a lip that will keep the sentence strips from slipping off the holder.

SENTENCE STRIP HOLDER

Use sentence strip holders to label objects around your classroom. The holders keep the labels visible, and help organize displays.

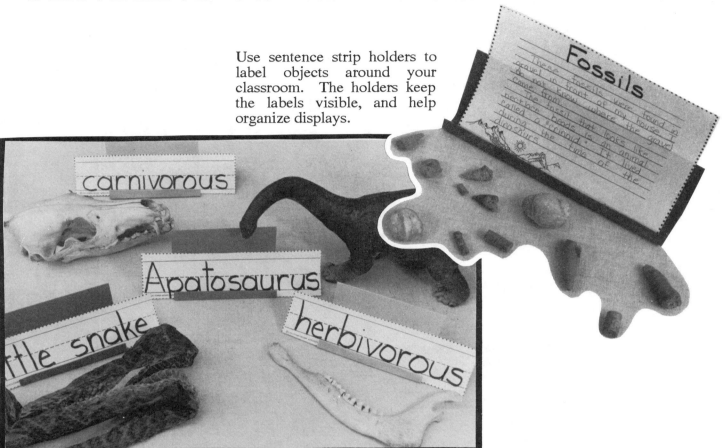

Teachers write and display notes to students.

Sentence strip holders can be used as pencil holders.

SENTENCE STRIP HOLDER

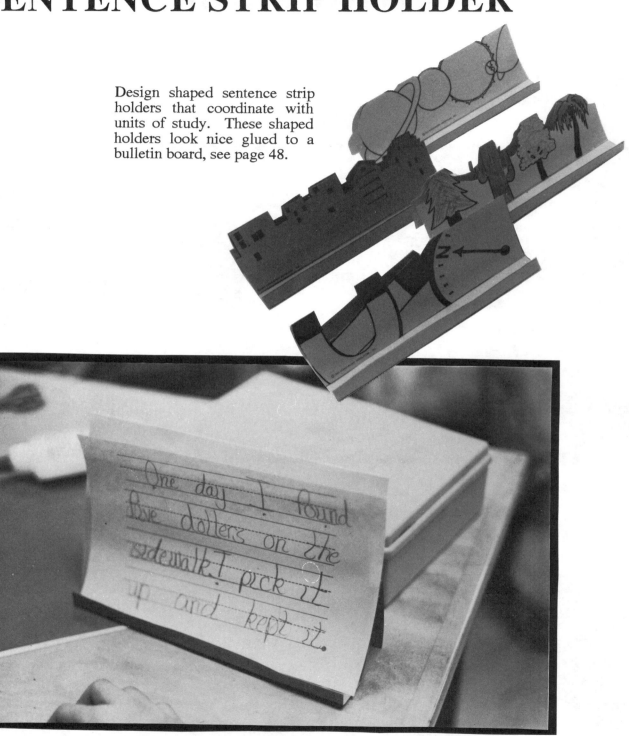

Design shaped sentence strip holders that coordinate with units of study. These shaped holders look nice glued to a bulletin board, see page 48.

Students collect and display their writing activities on these holders.

SENTENCE STRIP HOLDER

Contractions

Compound Words

Subject and Predicate Writing Activities

Vocabulary and spelling words can be stored inside the "tent" formed by this fold. Use word cards that are 1/5 of a sheet of 8 1/2" x 11" paper.

SENTENCE STRIP HOLDER

Cut sentence strip holders in half to make a place value activity.

Glue sentence strip holders to a paper-covered bulletin board to display student work, pictures, vocabulary words, and more. This makes it easy for students to read each other's work and then place it back on the sentence strip holder.

NOTE: Sentence strip holders cut in half are also perfect for displaying folded books, 3/4 books, vocabulary books, and question and answer books.

REPORT STAND FILE FOLDER

1. Convert a file folder into a report stand.

2. Cut downward at an angle two inches away from the center fold, until you are approximately two and one-half inches from the bottom. Turn the file folder and curve the cut upward about an inch forming an angle.

3. The cut should look like a large check mark. Open the fold for a sturdy picture or report stand holder.

Make small stands for half sheets of paper using an 8 1/2" x 11" piece of paper.

BOUND BOOKS
LARGE/REGULAR/SMALL

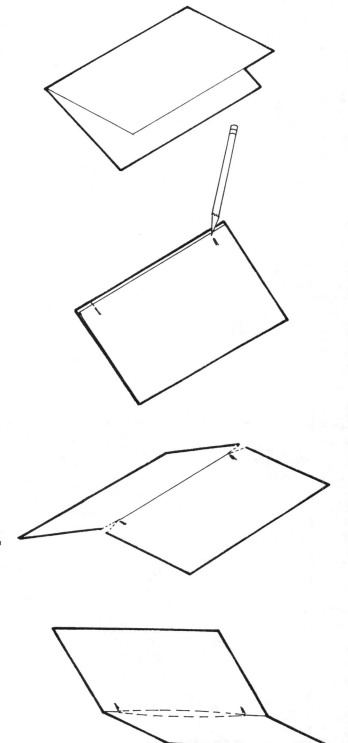

This book binding process was developed by scribes hundreds of years ago.

1. Take two sheets of paper (8 1/2" x 11") and separately fold them like a hamburger.

2. Place the folds side-by-side allowing 1/16" between the mountain tops.

3. Mark both folds 1" from the outer edges.*

4. On one of the folded sheets "cut up" from the top and bottom edge to the marked spot on both sides.

5. On the second folded sheet, start at one of the marked spots and "cut out" the fold between the two marks. Do not cut into the fold too deeply, only shave it off.

*For the young student, mark an index card at the 1" distance on both sides. The student can then lay the index card on top of the folds to mark the proper distance.

50

6. Take the "cut up" sheet and burrito it. Place the burrito through the "cut out" sheet and then open the burrito up. Fold the bound pages in half to form a book.

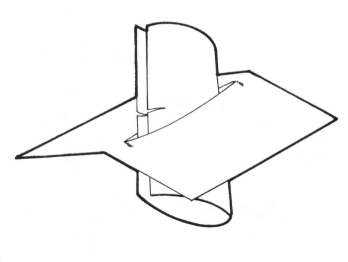

variation...

1. To make a larger book use additional sheets of paper marking each sheet as explained in #3.

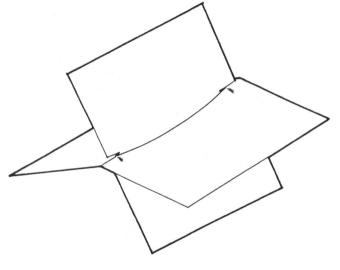

2. Use an equal number of sheets for the "cut up" and "cut out." Place them one on top of the other and follow directions 4 through 6.

3. Take a sheet of construction paper and fold it in half like a hamburger. Glue the front and back sheets of the bound book inside the construction paper hamburger to make a sturdy bound book.

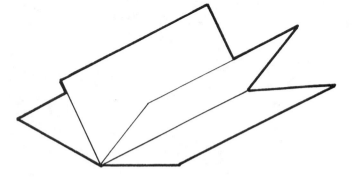

HINT:

Each single piece of paper folded in half makes a four page book. To make a twenty page book use five sheets of paper. If a book is glued inside a cover, the two outside pages will be lost. So remember, add an extra sheet for a twenty page book.

BOUND BOOKS
LARGE/REGULAR/SMALL

Make bound books filled with stories, poems, songs, riddles, current events, pictures, memorabilia, etc.

Use bound books for diaries, journals, observation books, experiment books, reports, creative writing, and more.

BOUND BOOKS
LARGE/REGULAR/SMALL

Make "big books" for the classroom using white butcher paper and poster board.

Glue student work inside. Students can use the paper found in the publishing center, page 8.

Students enjoy reading and rereading these books throughout the year.

DESK FILE PATTERN

1. Fold a sheet of paper (8 1/2" x 11") in half like a hamburger.

2. Fold the hamburger in half again like a hot dog forming fourths.

3. Fold in half again like a hot dog forming eighths.

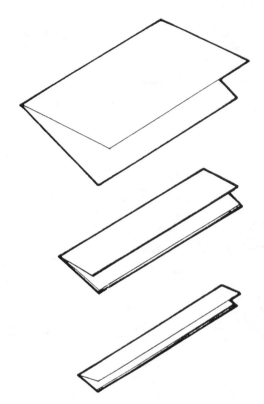

4. Open the folded sheet of paper and refold it like a fan. Crease the folds well. It is important that the folds are sharp.

5. Place the fan so that four mountains are pointing up and the three valleys are between the folds.

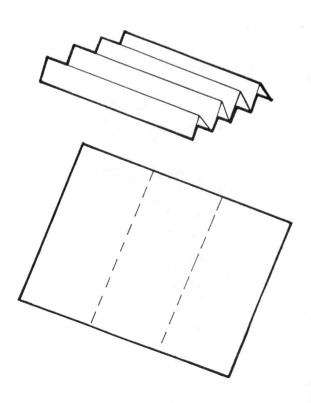

6. Fold another sheet of paper (8 1/2" x 11") into a trifold. Cut the paper along the fold lines leaving three separate, but equal sections.

DESK FILE PATTERN

7. Place these sections of paper into the desk file you just made. They will stand and allow you to organize work in sequence or they can be used for a beginning, middle, and ending format.

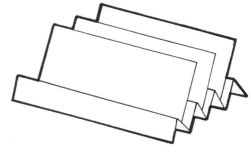

8. When not in use, fold desk file flat, place paper clips on the ends, and store.

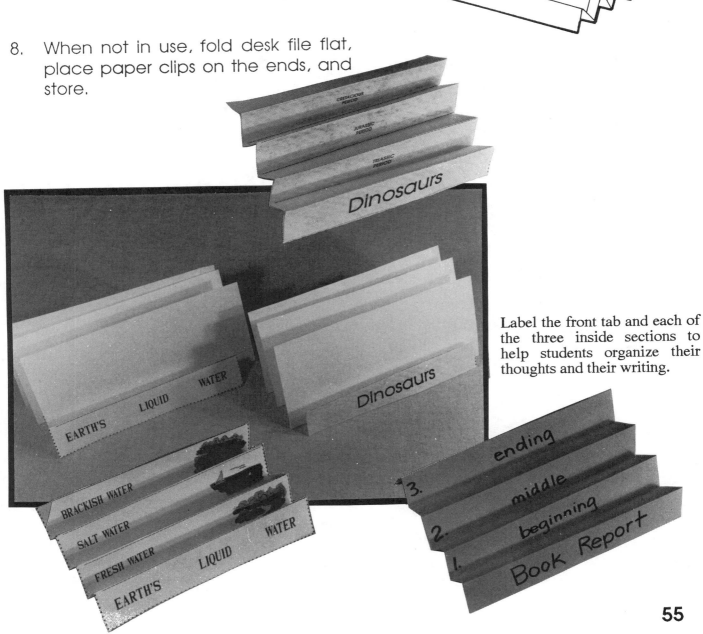

Label the front tab and each of the three inside sections to help students organize their thoughts and their writing.

DRINKING CUP POCKETS

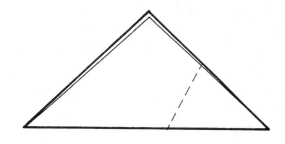

1. Take a sheet of paper (8 1/2" x 11") and fold into a taco forming a square. Cut off the excess paper strip formed by the fold.

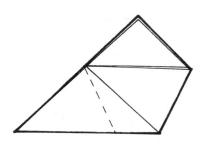

2. Leave the taco folded and place the peak upward. Fold the right corner toward the center left side. Then fold the left corner toward the center right side.

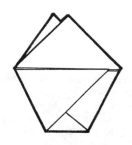

3. Separate the two peak tabs and fold each side downward toward the base.

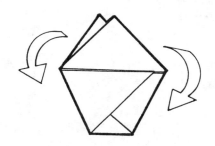

4. Open the pocket forming a drinking cup (that will actually hold water). Use to store vocabulary words on a bulletin board.

DRINKING CUP POCKETS

This cup really holds water. Scouting troops have used it for years!

Dixie's Cup

A small present can be hidden in this cup-basket, or use it for an Easter activity.

The cup can hold vocabulary words, and it makes a nice bulletin board.

BOX FOLD

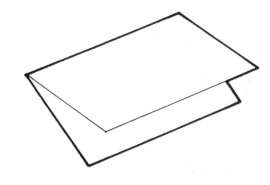

1. Fold two sheets of paper (8 1/2" x 11") in half like a hamburger.

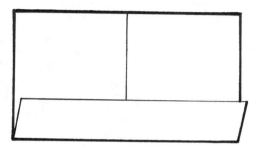

2. Open each folded sheet and fold one of the long sides up three inches and crease well.

3. Open each folded sheet again. Fold the outer edges in toward the valley forming two half inch tabs.

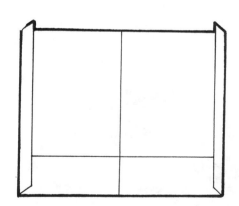

4. With the valleys of the two folds facing each other, glue the end tabs of one sheet to the end tabs of the other sheet. This forms an open ended cube.

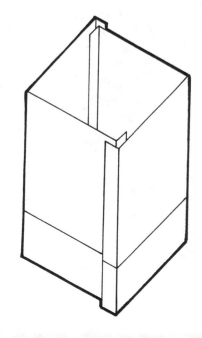

BOX FOLD

5. Cut each corner up to the three inch fold line.

6. Fold the flaps down to form the bottom of the box. Glue in place.

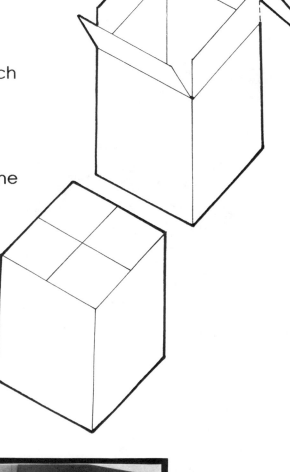

This box can be used to hold presents hidden in tissue paper!

BOX FOLD

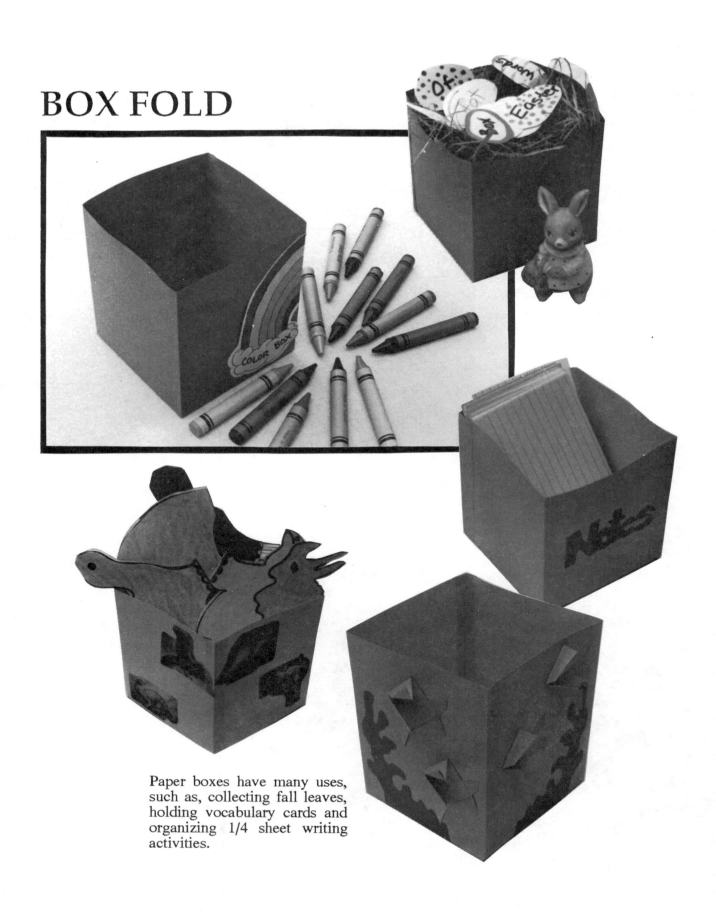

Paper boxes have many uses, such as, collecting fall leaves, holding vocabulary cards and organizing 1/4 sheet writing activities.

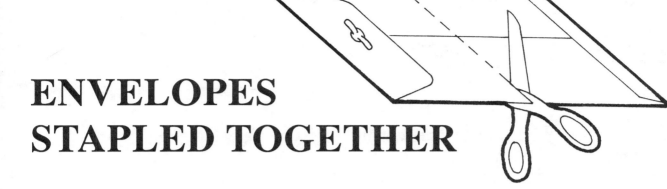

ENVELOPES STAPLED TOGETHER

1. Cut the flaps off several letter or legal size envelopes. Staple the envelopes together along one side and use as files for research information or pictures.

Envelopes can be used to organize writing and research or the steps in which something occurs, such as a story or science experiment.

Collect words that students have difficulty spelling and keep these cards available for reference.

BOOK JACKET

1. Fold a sheet of paper (8 1/2" x 11") in half like a hamburger, leaving one side a quarter of an inch shorter than the other side, then crease.

2. Move the shorter side up, making it a quarter of an inch longer than the previous long side, and crease. This will form a quarter inch spine in the center of the book.

3. Fold the outer edges toward the valley, forming two, one and a half inch tabs.

4. Fold the book jacket in half like a hamburger and cut along this fold to form two mini-book jackets.

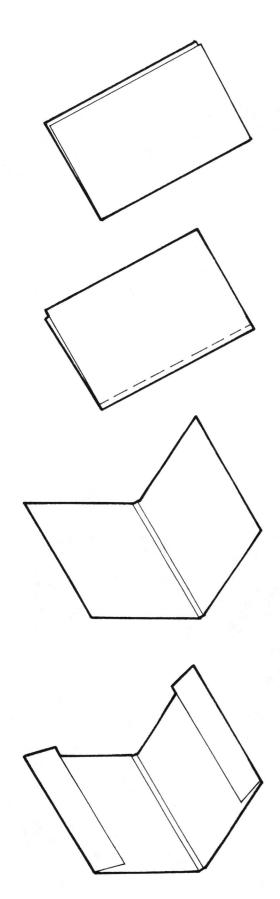

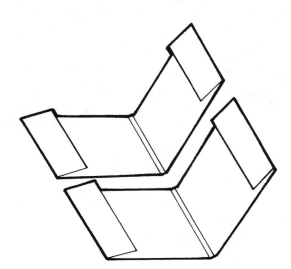

BOOK JACKET

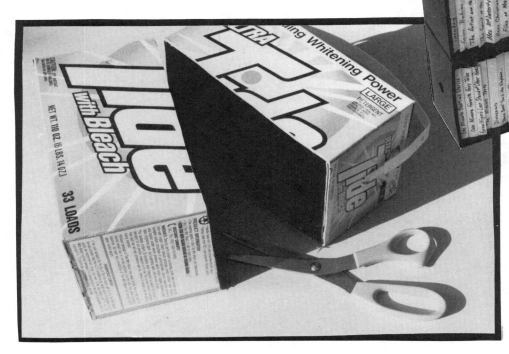

Make book shelves for the book jackets using the ends of a strong cardboard box glued together.

Note to teachers and parents: Make a book jacket for each book you read out loud to a child or student group.

Students write a brief synopsis of a book they have read inside the book jacket. They can rate the book according to their reaction to it:

   1 star = ok
   2 stars = good
   3 stars = great
   4 stars = fantastic

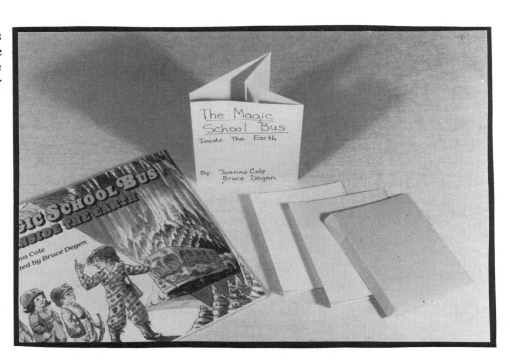

CIRCLE MOBILE AND BOOK

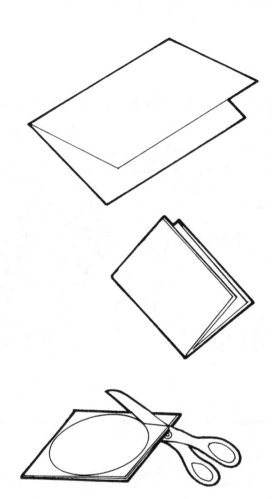

1. Fold a sheet of paper (8 1/2" x 11") in half like a hamburger. Fold again like a hamburger forming fourths.

2. Use a large glass or small saucer as a circle pattern. Trace a circle on one side of the folded paper. Cut around the outlined circle, leaving four individual circles.

3. Fold each circle in half, then fold in half again, forming fourths.

4. Use a marker to color the single fold edge of each folded circle.

5. Glue the folds together, matching the colored spines, side-by-side. Use a small amount of glue around all the edges of each fold.

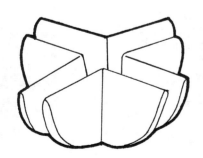

CIRCLE MOBILE
AND BOOK

6. When the sections are opened to show a half circle, students write on, or place labels on the half sections. These labels should correspond with the information or illustrations that will be visible when the entire circle is opened.

7. Open all half circles to form a three-dimensional ball of information.

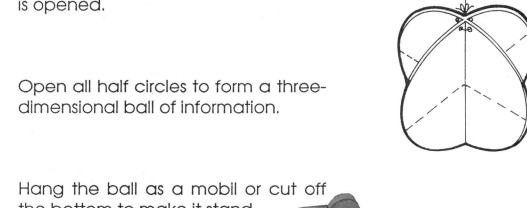

8. Hang the ball as a mobil or cut off the bottom to make it stand.

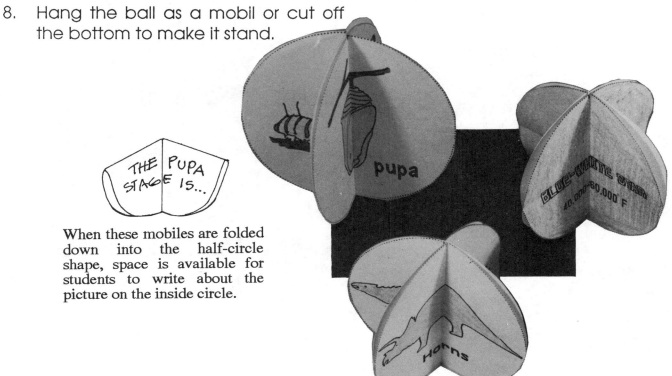

When these mobiles are folded down into the half-circle shape, space is available for students to write about the picture on the inside circle.

CIRCLE MOBILE AND BOOK

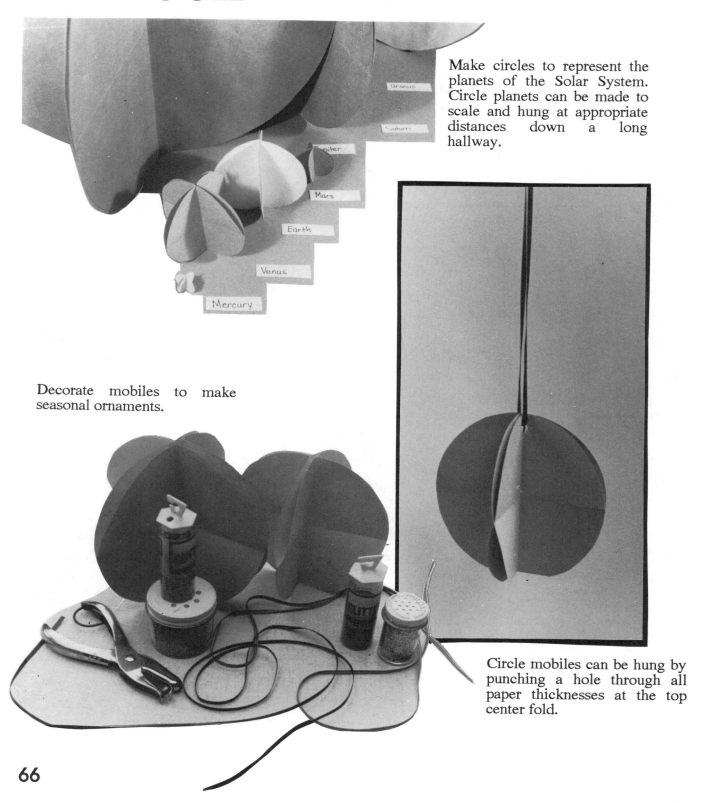

Make circles to represent the planets of the Solar System. Circle planets can be made to scale and hung at appropriate distances down a long hallway.

Uranus

Saturn

Jupiter

Mars

Earth

Venus

Mercury

Decorate mobiles to make seasonal ornaments.

Circle mobiles can be hung by punching a hole through all paper thicknesses at the top center fold.

ENVELOPE FOLD

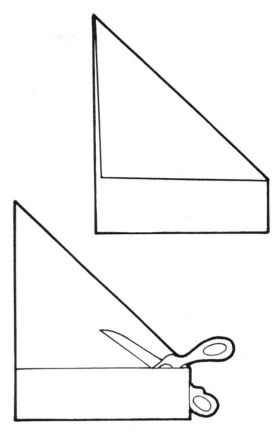

1. Fold a sheet of paper (8 1/2" x 11") into a taco forming a square. Cut off the excess paper strip formed by the fold.

2. Open the folded taco and refold it the opposite way forming another taco and an X fold pattern.

3. Open the taco fold and fold the corners toward the center point of the X forming a small square.

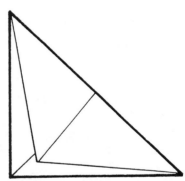

4. Trace this square on another sheet of paper. Cut and glue it to the inside of the envelope. Pictures can be placed under or on top of the tabs, or this fold can be used to teach fractional parts.

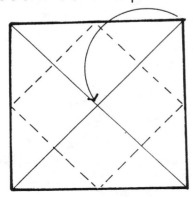
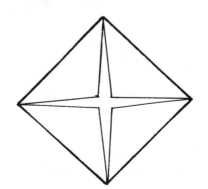
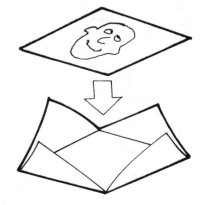

ENVELOPE FOLD

variation:

1. Write a letter or personal note and place inside the envelope fold.

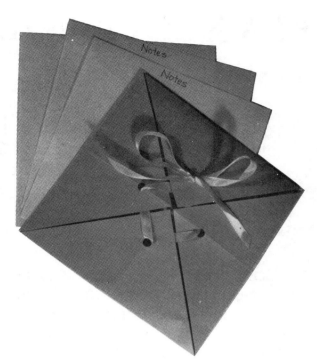

2. Punch holes in each end of the four corners and run yarn or ribbon through the holes. Finish off with a bow.

Stationery Packet
Great for presents or student writing activities.

3. Fill the envelope fold packet with small pieces of brightly colored stationary. This makes a nice gift.

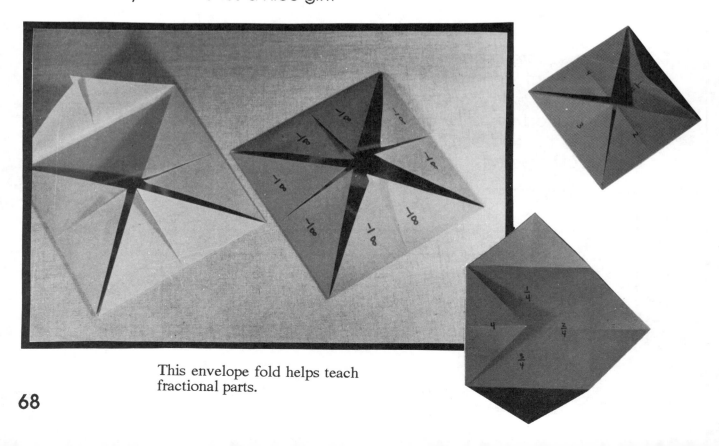

This envelope fold helps teach fractional parts.

ENVELOPE FOLD

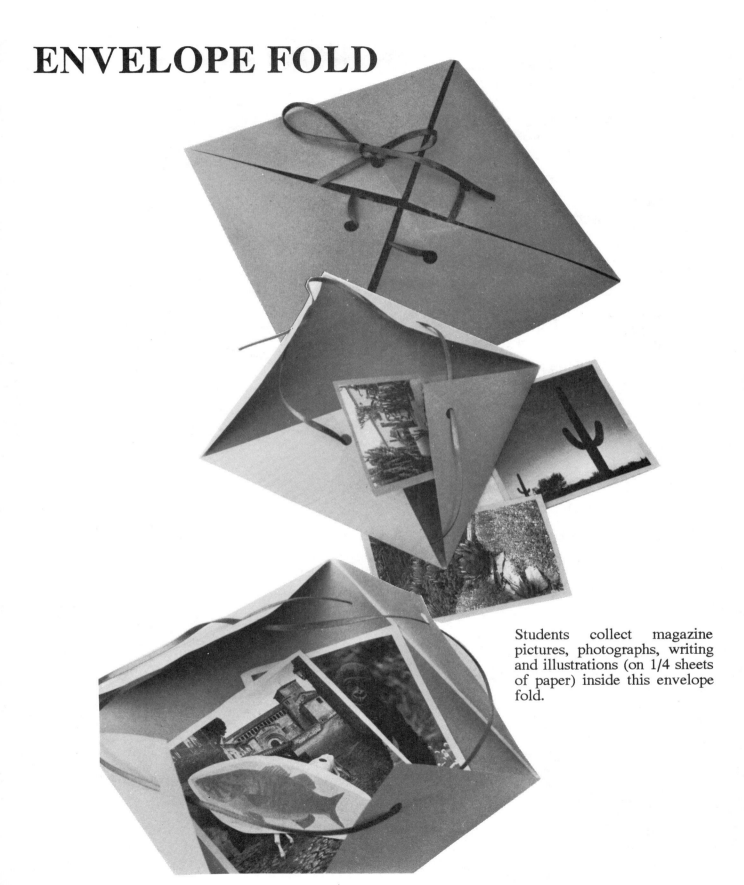

Students collect magazine pictures, photographs, writing and illustrations (on 1/4 sheets of paper) inside this envelope fold.

LAYERED LOOK BOOK

1. Stack two sheets of paper (8 1/2" x 11"), and place the back sheet one inch higher than the front sheet.

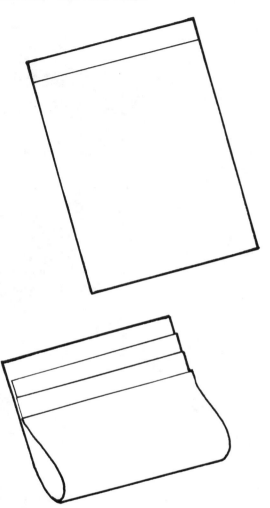

2. Bring the bottom of both sheets upward and align the edges so that all of the layers or tabs are the same distance apart.

3. When all tabs are an equal distance apart, fold the papers and crease well.

4. Open the papers and glue them together along the valley/center fold.

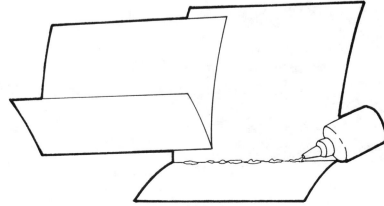

LAYERED LOOK BOOK

Use this layered look book to organize writing activities into beginning, middle and ending sections.

Place 13 sheets of paper 1/4" apart to form this vocabulary or spelling dictionary. Have students initial the words they add to the classroom book.

Make bulletin board layered look books out of bulletin board paper or butcher paper. Hang these giant classroom books on dowels suspended from the ceiling.

LAYERED LOOK BOOK

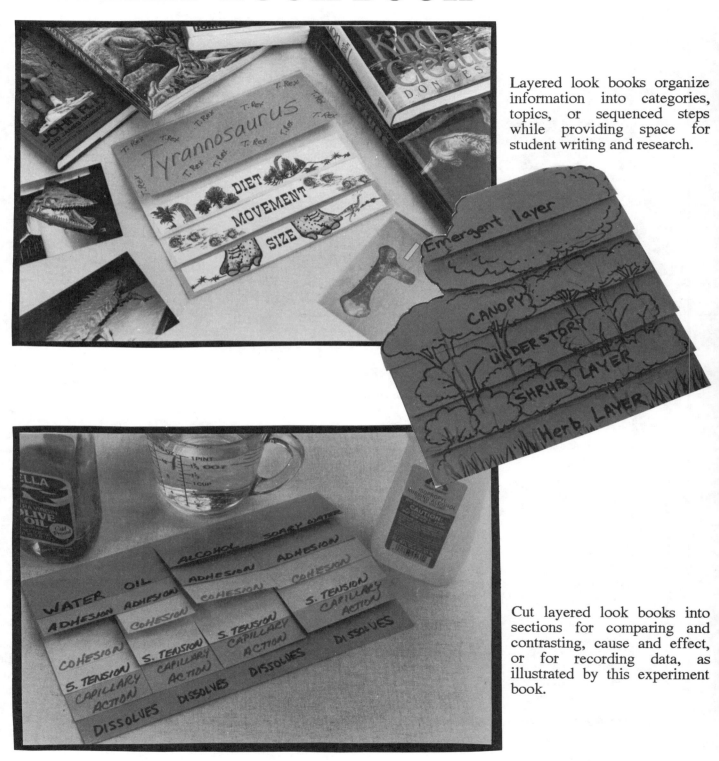

Layered look books organize information into categories, topics, or sequenced steps while providing space for student writing and research.

Cut layered look books into sections for comparing and contrasting, cause and effect, or for recording data, as illustrated by this experiment book.

LAYERED LOOK BOOK

These layered look books are action manipulatives as well as writing and research activities.

This book can also be used by older and more advanced students. They investigate the Earth's hydrosphere, lithosphere, atmosphere, and outer space beyond the exosphere.

LAYERED LOOK BOOK

Use layered look books to teach time, money, and measurement.

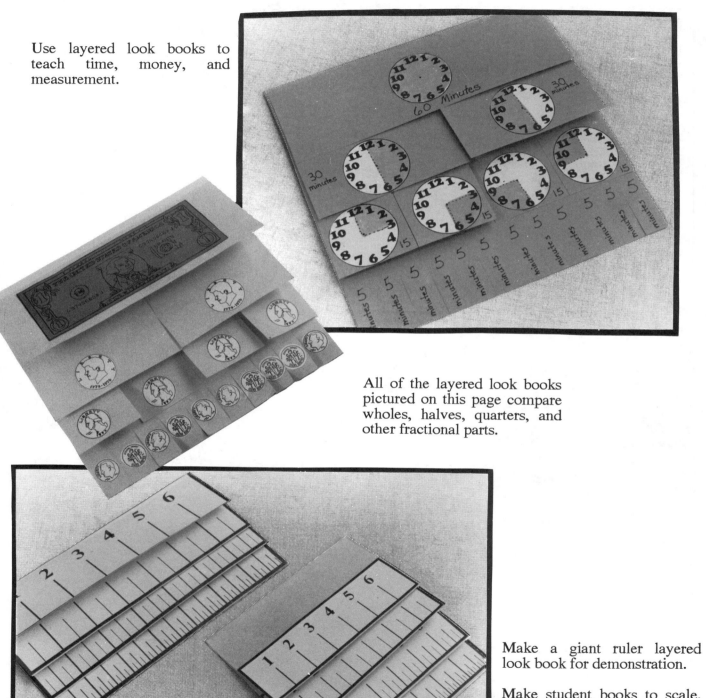

All of the layered look books pictured on this page compare wholes, halves, quarters, and other fractional parts.

Make a giant ruler layered look book for demonstration.

Make student books to scale. Students place an object to be measured on each ruler beginning with the inch ruler and progressing downward until they find the exact length of the object.

LAYERED LOOK BOOK

Layered look books make vertical and horizontal bar graphs.

Students write under the tabs, beside each graph bar, explaining the data being reported by the graph.

If students do not understand how to draw and color percentages on the bar graphs, use the money layered look book as an aid. For example: 46.6% is nearly a half-dollar, 27.72% is slightly more than a quarter, 8.13% is a little less than a dime, 5.0% is half of a dime, etc.

Use these graph books to integrate science, social studies, mathematics and language arts skills.

LAYERED LOOK BOOK

Cut a piece of 8 1/2″ x 11″ paper into thirds.

Fold as illustrated in the photograph. Use to teach ones and tens place value.

When appropriate, write information using the number on the back of the card to incorporate reading skills.

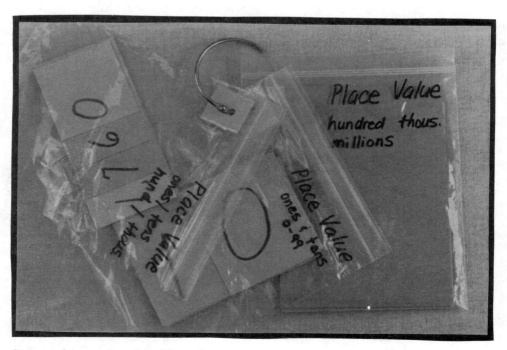

Store place-value booklets in quart-size plastic bags.

LAYERED LOOK BOOK

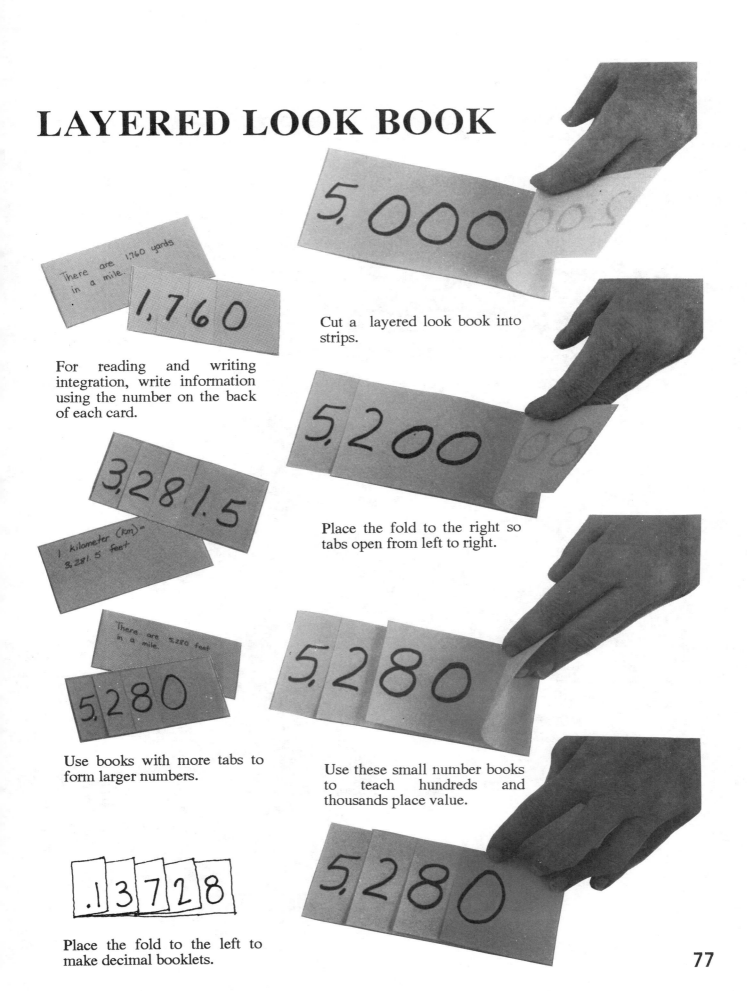

For reading and writing integration, write information using the number on the back of each card.

Use books with more tabs to form larger numbers.

Place the fold to the left to make decimal booklets.

Cut a layered look book into strips.

Place the fold to the right so tabs open from left to right.

Use these small number books to teach hundreds and thousands place value.

LAYERED LOOK BOOK

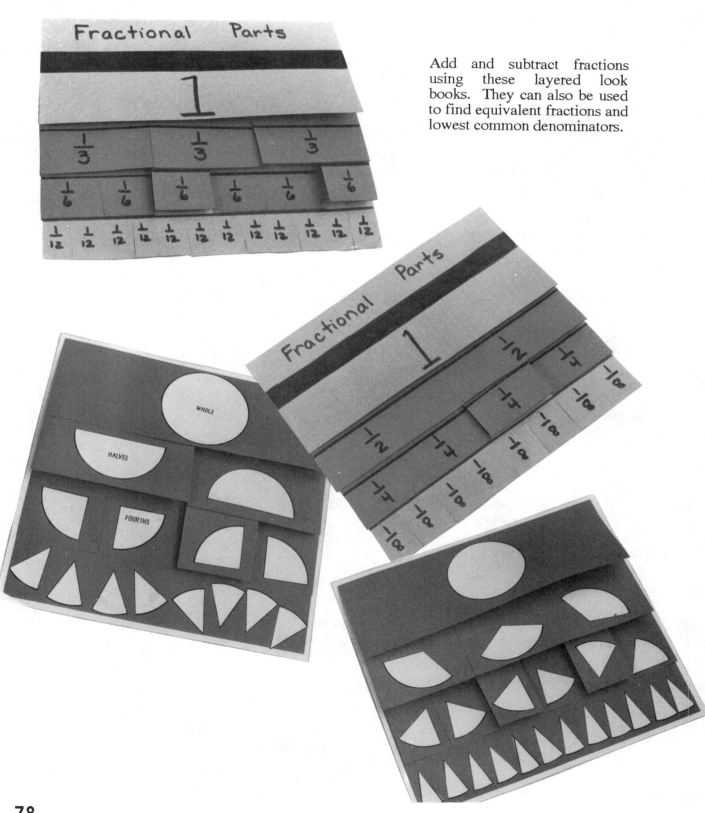

Add and subtract fractions using these layered look books. They can also be used to find equivalent fractions and lowest common denominators.

GIANT CRAYONS

This activity should be done with an adult helper.

1. Collect crayons and sort them by color. Remove all paper from the crayons.

2. Fill a 3 oz. paper cup with crayons of one color.

3. In a tin can melt additional crayons of the same color by placing the can in hot water. Do not stir.

4. Pour the melted crayon mixture over the crayons in the paper cup. Allow crayons to completely cool and remove from container.

variations:

1. To make mixed color crayons, fill the 3 oz. paper cup with two or three different colors. Some useful combinations are:

Brown, black and white = Land
Blues and white = Sky
Blues and greens = Water
Different shades of green = Trees
Red, yellow, orange = Fire, Lava or Sun
Brown, white, beige = Sand, Desert or Beach

2. Pour melted crayon wax into candy molds to make shaped crayons.

TOP TAB BOOKS

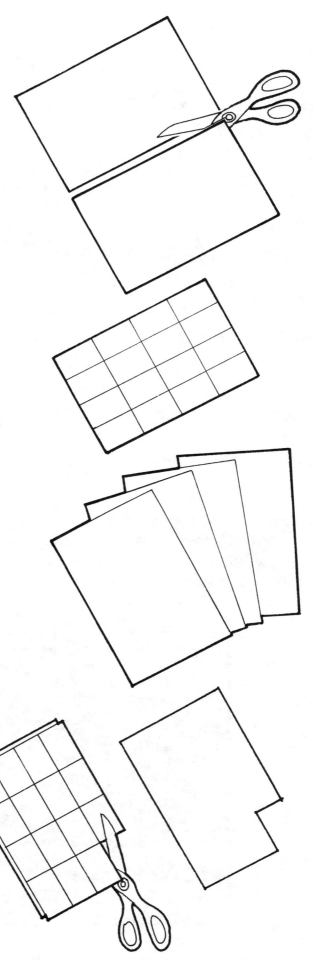

1. Fold a sheet of paper (8 1/2" x 11") in half like a hamburger. Cut the center fold forming two half sheets.

2. Fold one of the half sheets four times. Begin by folding in half like a hamburger, fold again like a hot dog, fold again like a hamburger, and finally again like a hamburger. This fold has formed your pattern of 4 rows of 4 small squares.

3. Fold 2 sheets of paper (8 1/2" x 11") in half like a hamburger. Cut the center folds forming four half sheets.

4. Hold the pattern vertically and place on a half sheet of paper under the pattern. Cut the bottom right hand square out of both sheets. Set this first page aside.

TOP TAB BOOKS

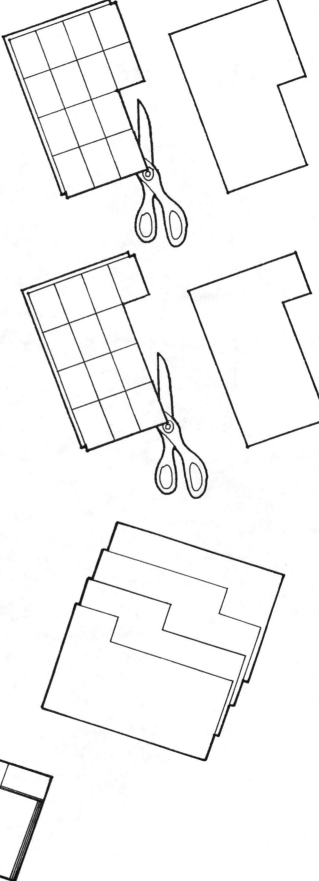

5. Take a second half sheet of paper and place it under the pattern. Cut the first and second right hand squares out of both sheets. Place the second page on top of the first page.

6. Take a third half sheet of paper and place it under the pattern. Cut the first, second, and third right hand squares out of both sheets. Place this third page on top of the second page.

7. Place the fourth half sheet of paper behind the three cut out sheets leaving four aligned tabs across the top of the book. Staple several times on the left side.

TOP TAB BOOKS

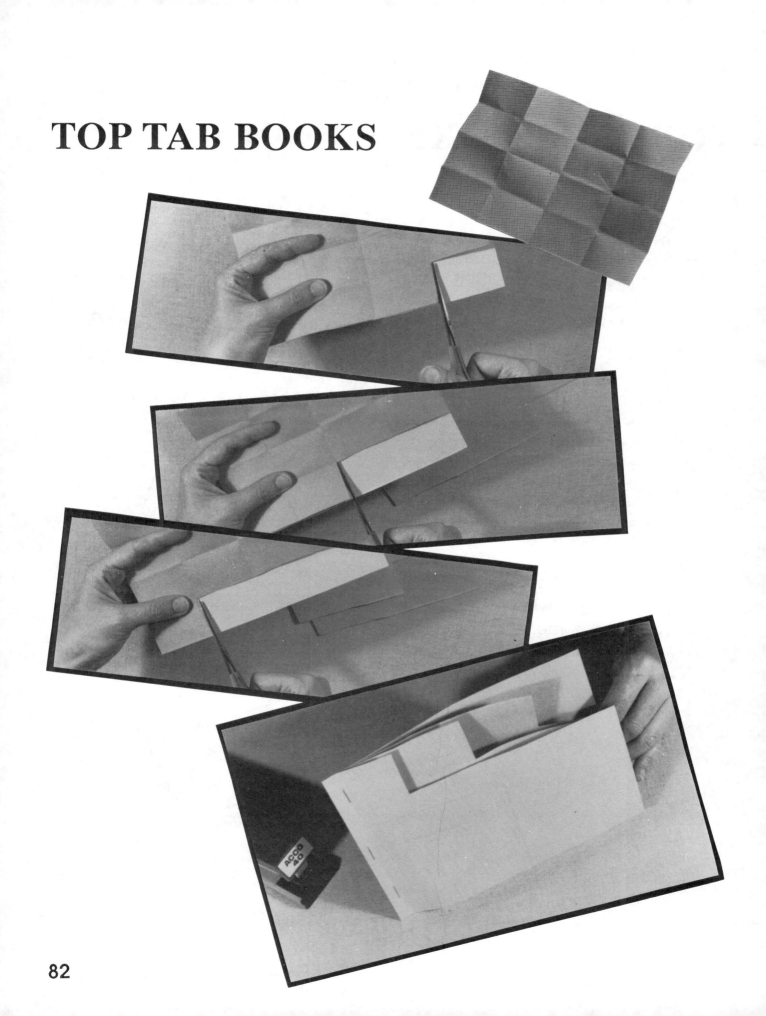

TOP TAB BOOKS

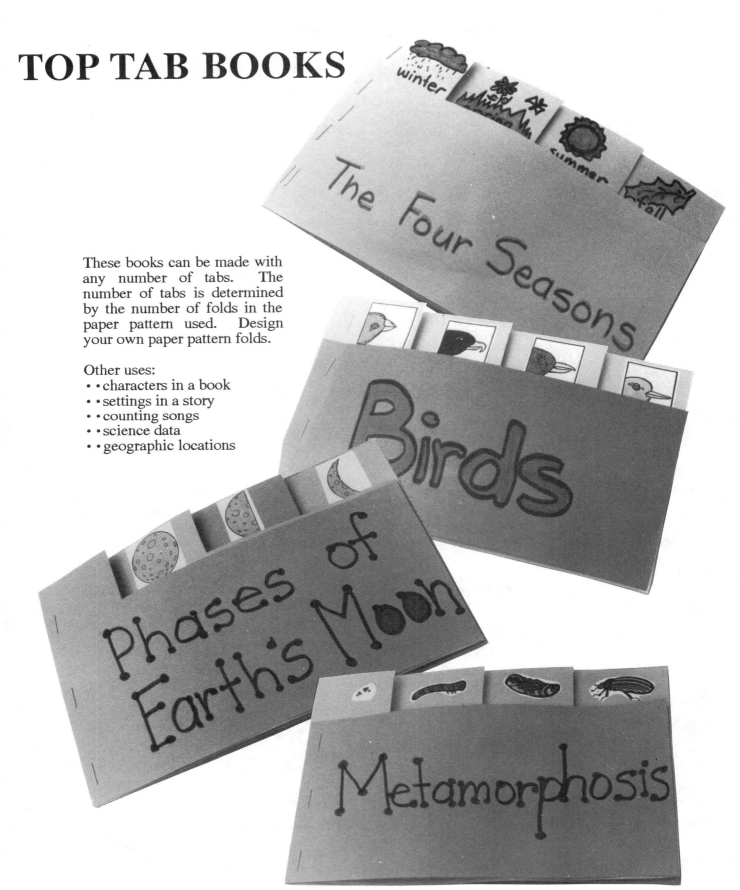

These books can be made with any number of tabs. The number of tabs is determined by the number of folds in the paper pattern used. Design your own paper pattern folds.

Other uses:
- • characters in a book
- • settings in a story
- • counting songs
- • science data
- • geographic locations

TRIFOLD BOOK

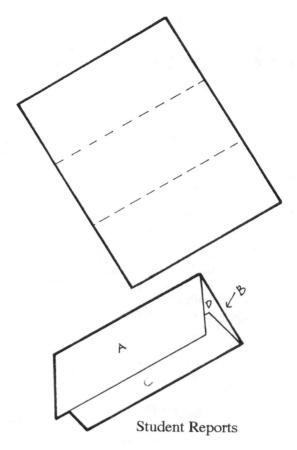

1. Fold a sheet of paper (8 1/2" x 11") into thirds.

2. Use this book as is, or cut into shapes. If the trifold is cut, leave plenty of fold on both sides of the designed shape, so the book will open and close in three sections.

Student Reports

A. Title on the front of the book.
B. About the author with a photograph on the back.
C. Vocabulary words on the inside flap.
D. Beginning, middle an ending writing activity inside.

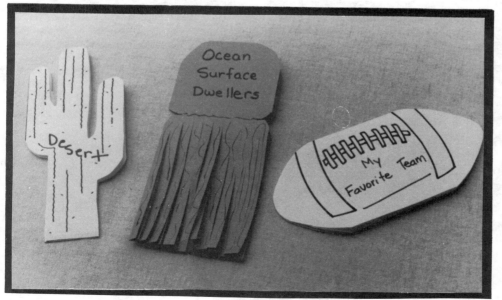

These are examples of trifold books originally designed by students.

TRIFOLD BOOK

Organize reports and creative writing projects into beginning, middle, and ending sections.

Trifold books make thematic question and answer bulletin boards. Write a question on the front, a hint on the inside flap, and the answer on the inside back section.

TRIFOLD BOOK

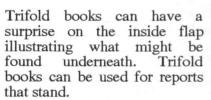

Trifold books can have a surprise on the inside flap illustrating what might be found underneath. Trifold books can be used for reports that stand.

TRIFOLD BOOK

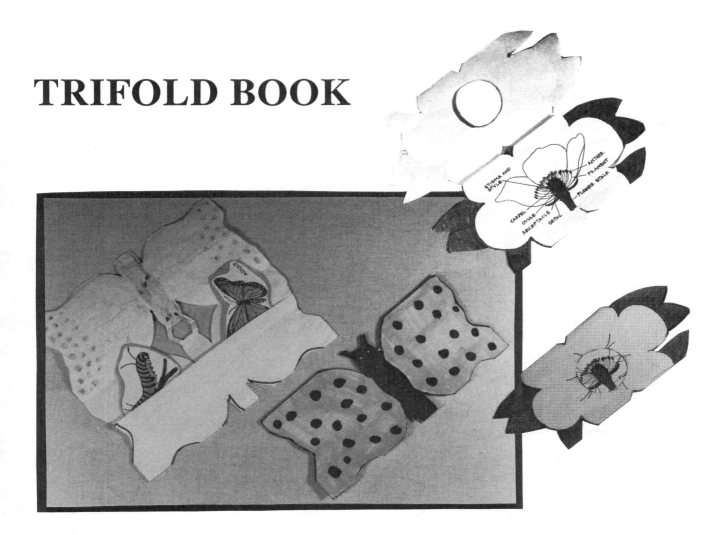

Cut the inside flap of a trifold book in half and glue it around the edges to form an open pocket. Fill the pocket with pictures, sentences, or words.

SINGLE PICTURE FRAME BOOK

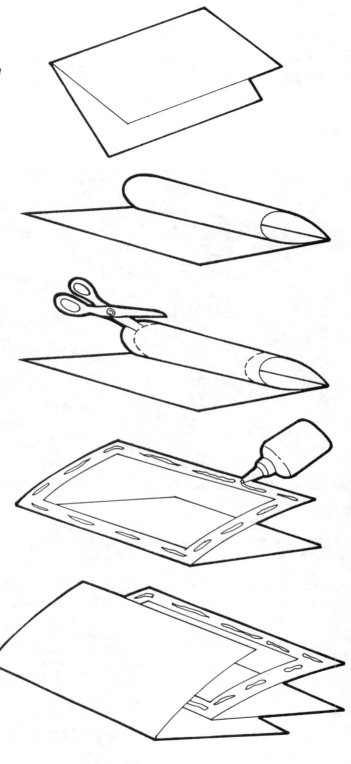

1. Fold a sheet of paper (8 1/2" x 11") in half like a hamburger.

2. Open the hamburger and gently roll one side of the hamburger toward the valley. Try not to crease the roll.

3. Cut a rectangle out of the middle of the rolled side of paper leaving a 1/2" border and forming a frame.

4. Fold another sheet of paper (8 1/2" x 11") in half like a hamburger.

5. Apply glue to the picture frame and place inside the hamburger fold.

variation:

1. Place a picture behind the frame and glue the edges of the frame to the other side of the hamburger fold. This locks the picture in place.

2. Cut out only 3 sides of the rolled rectangle. This forms a window with a cover that opens and closes.

SINGLE PICTURE
FRAME BOOK

The single picture frame book focuses on one picture and provides three pages for writing.

This picture illustrates variation 2 described on page 88. A report, description, information, or a story is written under the flap.

DOUBLE PICTURE
FRAME BOOK

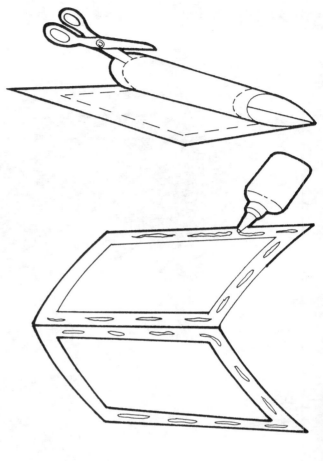

1. Follow directions 1 through 3 of the Single Picture Book, but roll and cut both sides of the hamburger fold.

2. Fold a sheet of construction paper in half like a hamburger. It is important to use strong paper to help secure the double frame and to give the book a border.

3. Place glue around three of the outer edges of the double frame and along the center fold. Do not glue the top. This will allow half sheets of paper to be slipped in and out of each frame. This book can be laminated for durability.

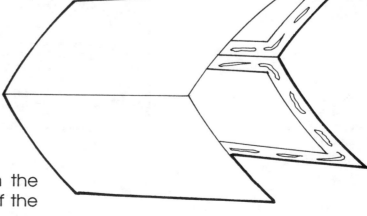

variation:

1. Glue half sheets of paper from the publishing center to the back of the double picture frame forming a permanent display.

DOUBLE PICTURE
FRAME BOOK

Make a double picture frame to display student work on half sheets of writing paper from the publishing center.

Frame student art work or coloring book pictures.

CENTER TAB FOLD

1. Fold a sheet of paper (8 1/2" x 11") in half like a hot dog.

2. Fold one side of the hot dog back toward the mountain top forming a center tab.

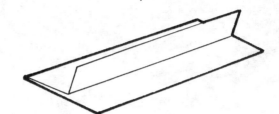

3. Glue the tab to the base.

4. Cut the tab into eight sections by first cutting the tab in half forming two tabs. Then cut the two tabs in half forming fourths. Finally, cut the fourths in half forming eighths.

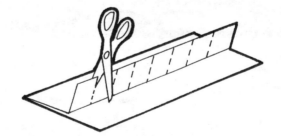

variation:

1. Make several center tab folds and cut the tabs into fractional parts: halves, fourths, sixths, eighths, etc.

CENTER TAB FOLD

Use these tab books for number sense activities. For example, calculate 68 - 14 as fast as you can in your head and write the answer under the tab.

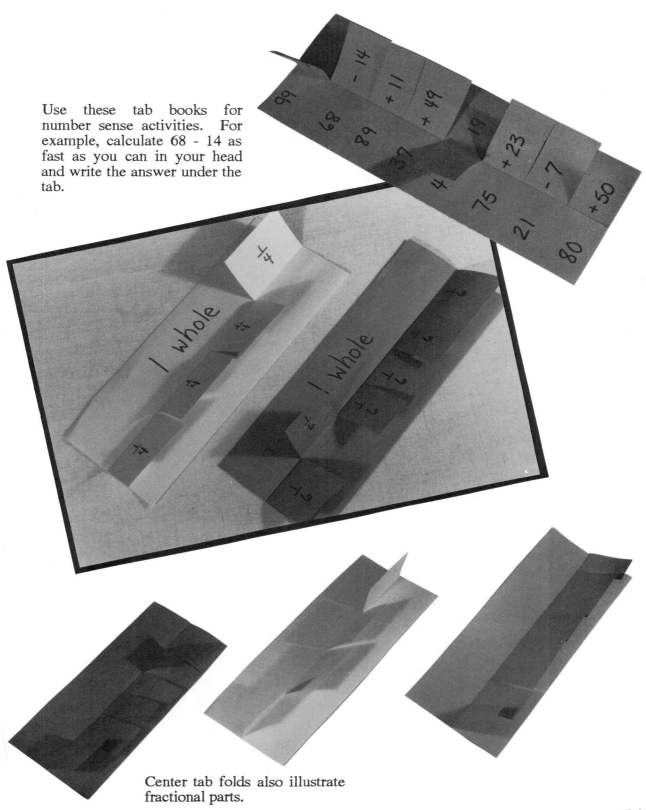

Center tab folds also illustrate fractional parts.

LARGE SENTENCE STRIPS

1. Take two sheets of paper (8 1/2" x 11") and fold into hamburgers. Cut along the fold lines making four half sheets. (Use as many half sheets as necessary for additional pages to your book.)

2. Fold each half sheet in half like a hot dog.

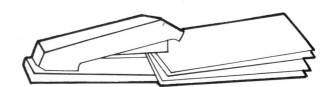

3. Place the folds side-by-side and staple them together on the left side.

4. 1" from the stapled edge, cut the front page of each folded section up to the mountain top. These cuts form flaps that can be raised and lowered.

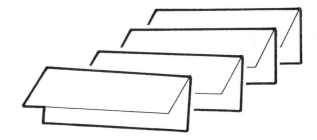

5. To make a half-cover, use a sheet of construction paper one inch longer than the book. Glue the back of the last sheet to the construction paper strip leaving one inch, on the left side, to fold over and cover the original staples. Staple this half-cover in place.

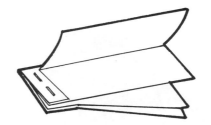

LARGE SENTENCE STRIPS

variation:

1. Use the same process as described for the "Large Sentence Strips," except begin with quarter sheets of paper. When completed, these books will be half the size of the large sentence strips.

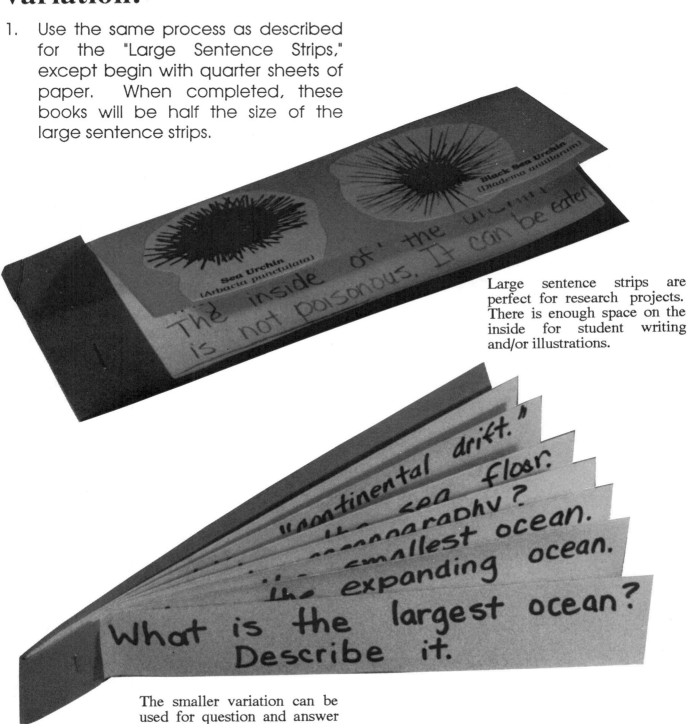

Large sentence strips are perfect for research projects. There is enough space on the inside for student writing and/or illustrations.

The smaller variation can be used for question and answer activities.

16 WORD VOCABULARY BOOKS

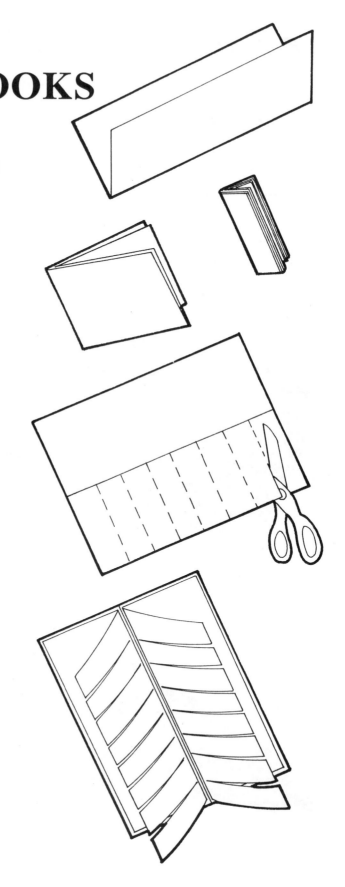

1. Take two sheets of paper (8 1/2" x 11") and fold each sheet like a hot dog.

2. Fold each hot dog in half like a hamburger. Fold the hamburger in half two more times and crease well. Open up the fold, and the sheet of paper will be divided into 1/16's.

3. On one side only, cut up the folds to the mountain top, forming eight tabs. Repeat this process on the second fold.

4. Take a sheet of construction paper and fold like a hot dog. Glue the solid back side of one vocabulary sheet, to one of the inside sections of the construction paper. Glue the second vocabulary sheet to the other side of the construction paper fold. (This step can be eliminated to form a one sided vocabulary book.) Make sure the center folds of the vocabulary books meet at the center fold of the construction paper.

16 WORD VOCABULARY BOOKS

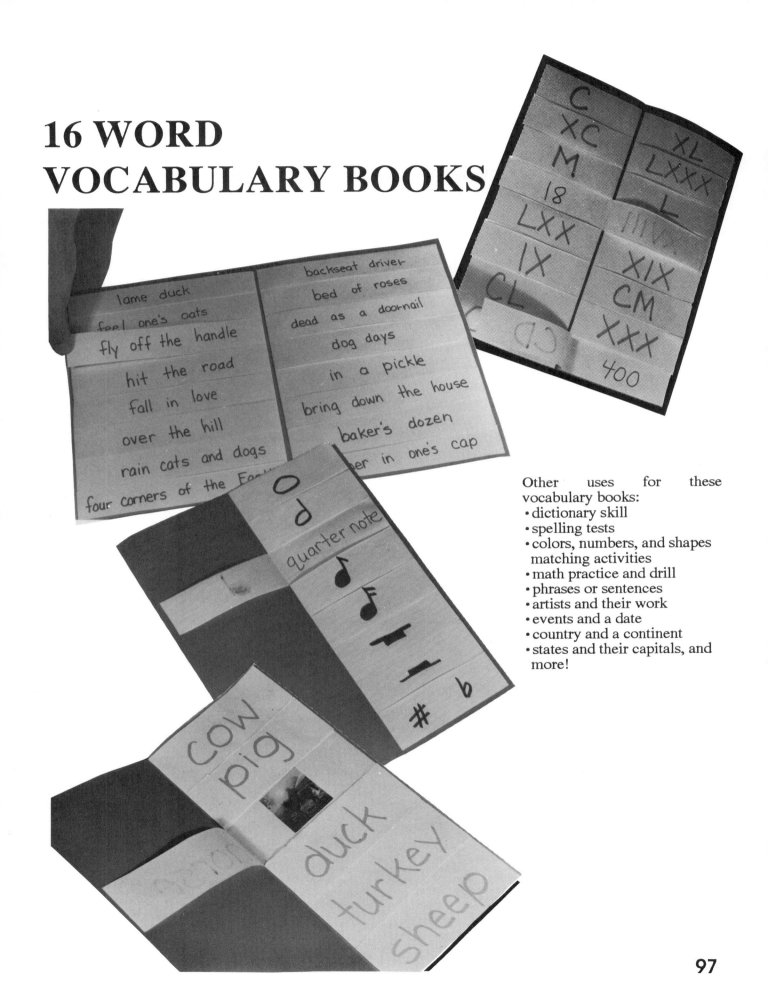

lame duck
feel one's oats
fly off the handle
hit the road
fall in love
over the hill
rain cats and dogs
four corners of the Earth

backseat driver
bed of roses
dead as a doornail
dog days
in a pickle
bring down the house
baker's dozen
...er in one's cap

C
XC   XL
M   LXXX
18   L
LXX   ...
IX   XIX
CL   CM
CD   XXX
      400

O
d
quarter note

cow
pig
duck
turkey
sheep

Other uses for these vocabulary books:
- dictionary skill
- spelling tests
- colors, numbers, and shapes matching activities
- math practice and drill
- phrases or sentences
- artists and their work
- events and a date
- country and a continent
- states and their capitals, and more!

SMALL QUESTION AND ANSWER BOOK

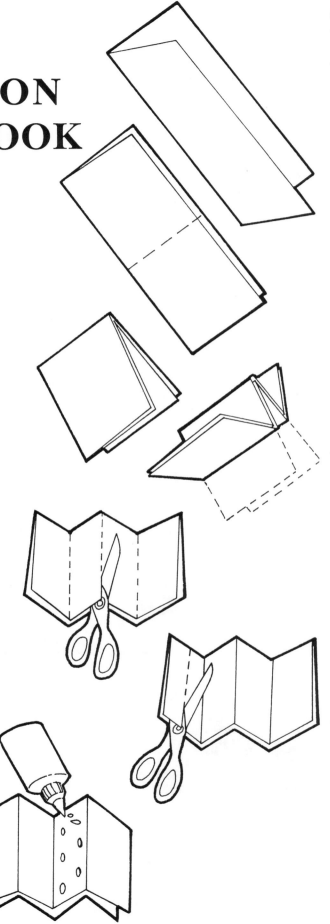

1. Fold a sheet of paper (8 1/2" x 11") in half like a hot dog.

2. Fold this long rectangle in half like a hamburger.

3. Fold both ends back to touch the mountain top.

4. On the side forming two valleys and one mountain top, make vertical cuts through one thickness of paper, forming tabs for questions and answers. These four tabs can also be cut in half making eight tabs.

5. Turn the book over to the side without cuts. Place glue on the two center sections and press together. Glue a cover on your book or make a longer question and answer book by gluing several books together "side-by-side."

SMALL QUESTION AND ANSWER BOOK

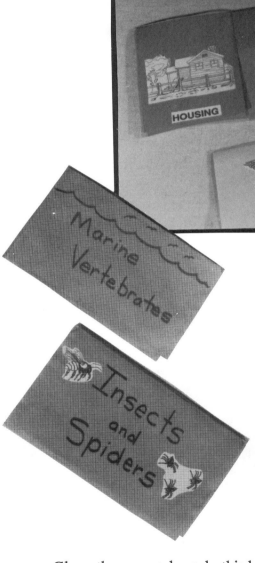

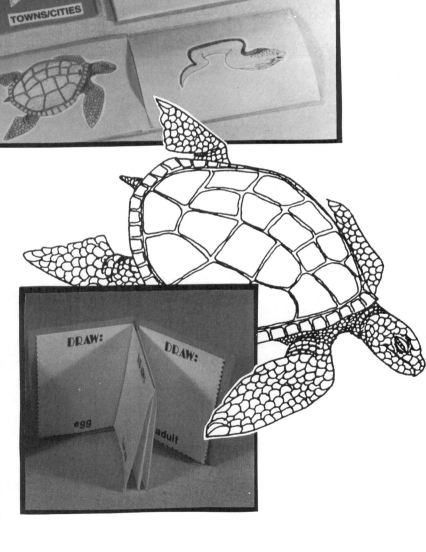

Glue the second and third sections of the back of a small question and answer book together to make these bound books. Several books can be glued side-by-side to make a larger book.

SMALL QUESTION
AND ANSWER BOOK

Use question and answer books for sequencing science information or the events in a story.

Front Cover

Back Cover

SMALL QUESTION AND ANSWER BOOK

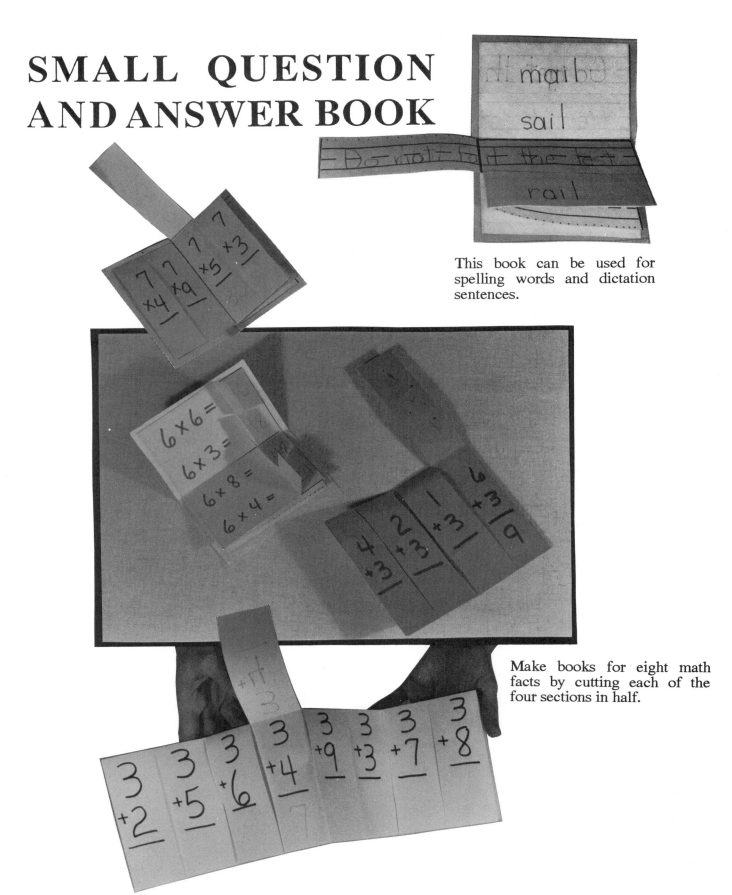

This book can be used for spelling words and dictation sentences.

Make books for eight math facts by cutting each of the four sections in half.

ACCORDION BOOK

1. Fold a sheet of paper (8 1/2" x 11") in half like a hot dog.

2. Fold this long rectangle in half like a hamburger.

3. Fold both ends back to touch the mountain top fold.

4. Place the book where you see one mountain top and two valleys. Glue a picture to the front and one to the back forming a beginning and an ending book cover.

ACCORDION BOOK

The fold of an accordion book goes up, and students write on the side with one mountain and two valleys.

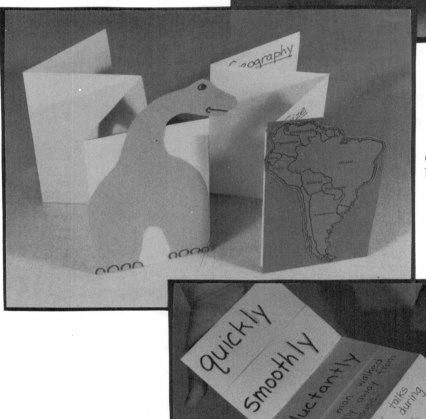

Glue a cover to the front and back of the accordion book.

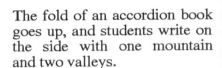

Each of the four sections can be cut in half forming eight small tabs. These can be used for vocabulary, spelling, math activities, and more.

ACCORDION BOOK

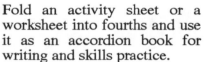

Fold an activity sheet or a worksheet into fourths and use it as an accordion book for writing and skills practice.

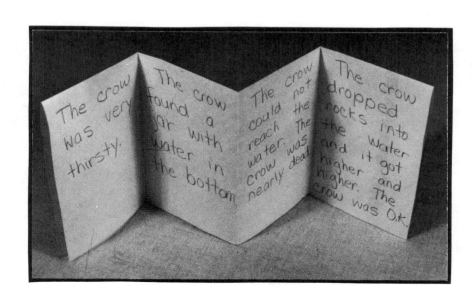

PATCH WORD QUILT SQUARE

1. Fold a sheet of paper (8 1/2" x 11") into a taco forming a square. Cut off the excess paper strip formed by the fold.

2. Open the folded taco and refold it the opposite way forming another taco and an X fold pattern.

3. Hold the taco flat, so that it looks like a mountain with the long side of the triangle forming the base of the mountain, and the top the peak.

4. Cut up the center of the mountain from the base toward the peak. Stop one inch from the peak.

5. Refold the taco along the other fold of the X pattern, and cut up the center of the mountain from the base toward the peak again. Stop one inch from the peak.

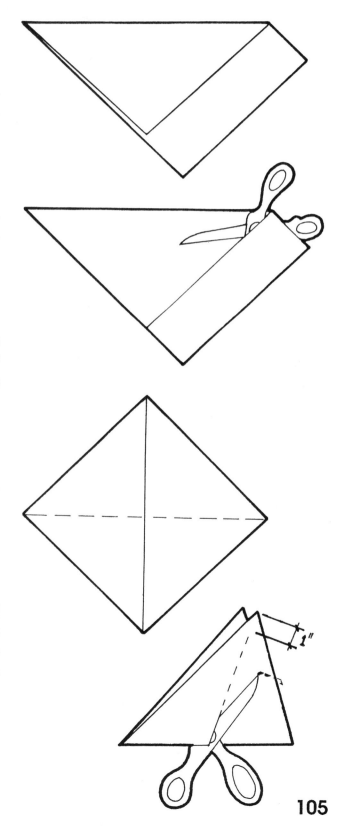

PATCH WORD QUILT SQUARE

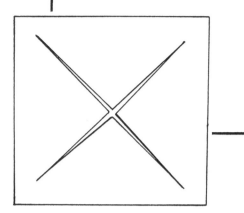

6. The cuts will form an X in the middle of the square.

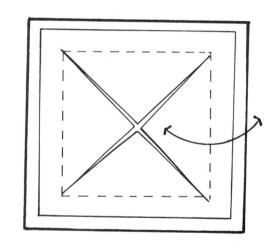

7. Place a small amount of glue around the outer edges of the square, then glue it onto a slightly larger construction paper square.

8. Fold the four triangular tabs formed, back and forth, to form windows. This hides whatever is glued or written underneath on the construction paper.

variation:

1. After step 5, cut off 1/2" of the mountain peak.

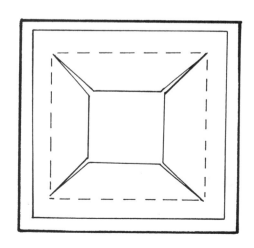

2. Glue onto a construction paper square.

3. This quilt square will have a small square in the center. This space can be used for writing words or numbers.

PATCH WORD QUILT SQUARE

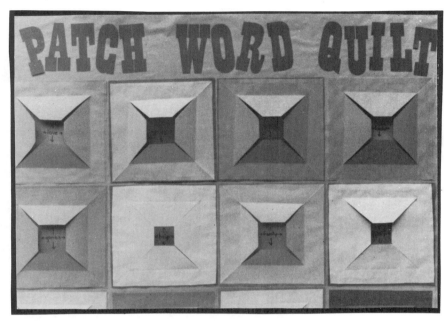

Warm up a wall with this patch word quilt bulletin board.

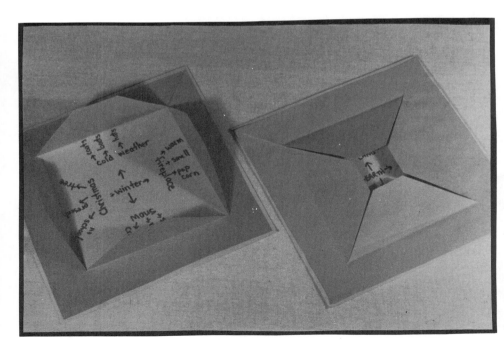

Use quilt squares for word webs. Vocabulary words from science, social studies, and literature can be placed in the center of the web.

PATCH WORD QUILT SQUARE

Place a picture behind the four tabs. Number the tabs as to the order in which they are to be raised. How quickly can a student identify the hidden picture?

Teach the compass rose and intermediate coordinates with these squares.

Use the squares to report on literature.

PATCH WORD QUILT SQUARE

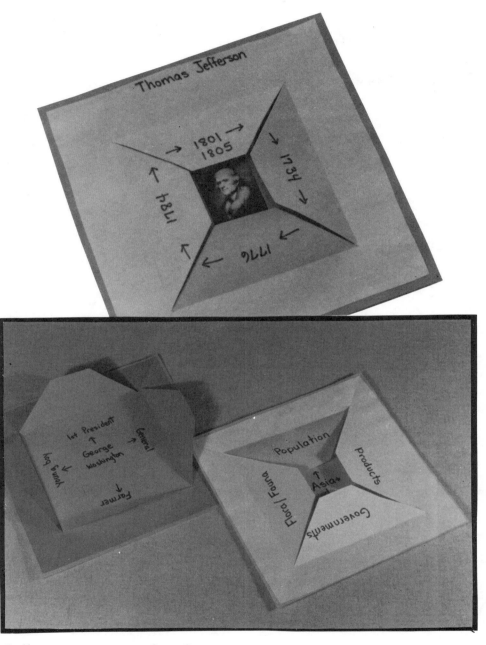

Quilt squares are perfect for reports on historical figures, cities, states, nations, continents and other social studies topics.

PAPER FILE FOLDERS

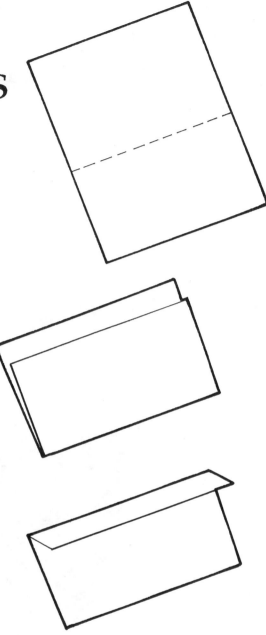

1. Fold four sheets of paper (8 1/2" x 11") in half like a hamburger. Leave one side 1" longer than the other side.

2. On each sheet, fold the one inch tab over the short side, forming an envelope-like fold.

3. Place the four sheets side-by-side, then move each fold so that the tabs are exposed.

4. Moving left to right, cut staggered tabs in each fold, two and one eighth inches wide. Fold the tabs upward.

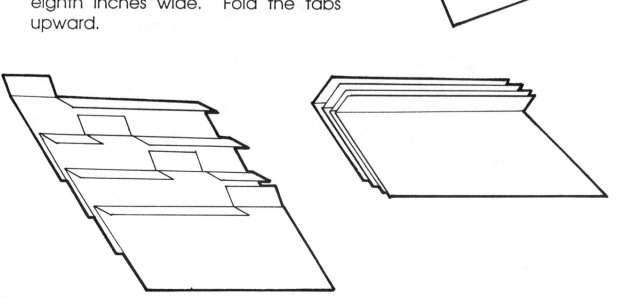

PAPER FILE FOLDERS

Collect sentences from literature that demonstrate these parts of speech.

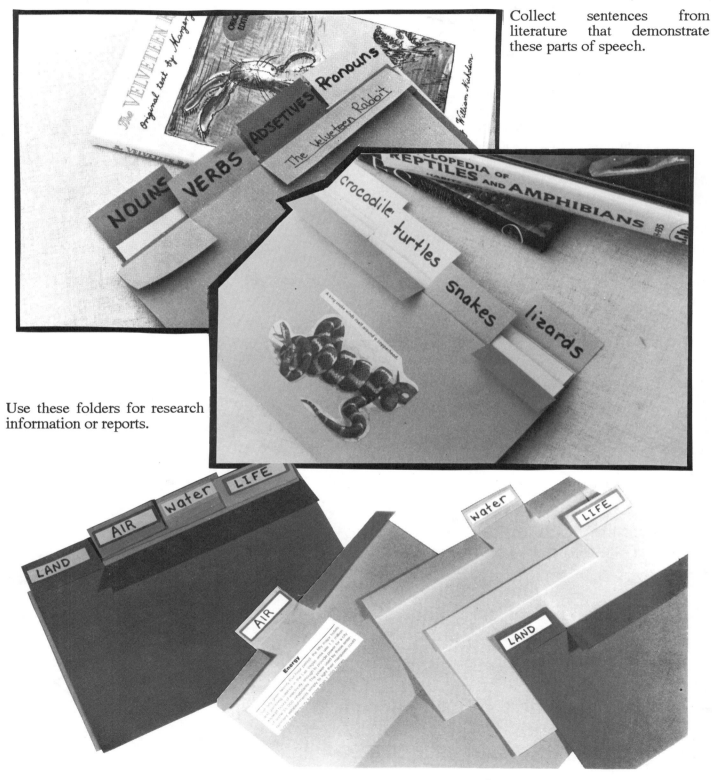

Use these folders for research information or reports.

Glue current events and articles inside the folders.

POP-UP BOOKS

Dinah's Rule for Pop-Up Books:
Always cut on a fold, never glue on a fold.

1. Fold a sheet of paper (8 1/2" x 11") in half like a hamburger.

2. Beginning at the fold, or mountain top, cut one or more tabs.

3. Fold the tabs back and forth several times until there is a good fold line formed.

4. Partially open the hamburger fold and push the tabs through to the inside.

5. With one small dot of glue, place figures for the Pop-Up Book to the front of each tab. Allow the glue to dry before going on to the next step.

6. To make a cover for the book, fold a sheet of construction paper in half like a hamburger.

7. Place glue around the outside edges of the Pop-Up Book and firmly press inside the construction paper hamburger.

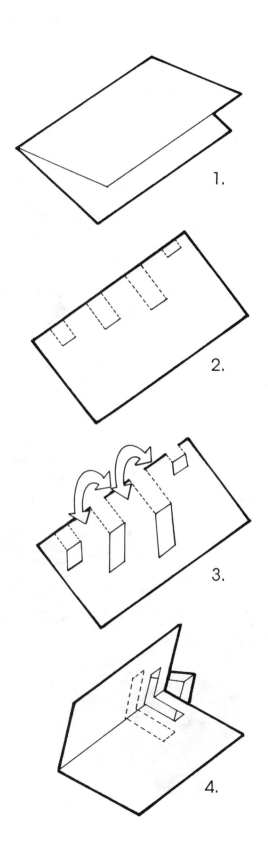

1.

2.

3.

4.

POP-UP BOOKS

variation:

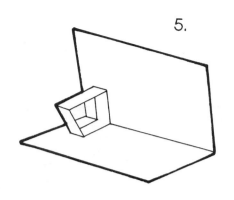

5.

1. To make a multi-paged Pop-Up Book, glue several Pop-Up folds side-by-side. Follow with a construction paper cover.

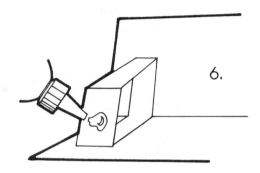

6.

2. To make a **diorama**, cut several tabs different lengths to make the picture dimensional. Use this same diorama cut to make a pop-up graph. See the illustration on page 115.

7.

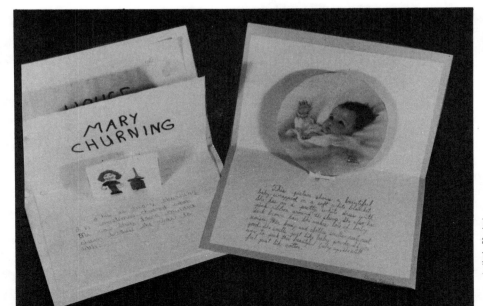

Pop-up books are perfect for student reports. Glue pop-up pages "side-by-side" to make longer books.

POP-UP BOOKS

Make pop-up book dictionaries or encyclopedias by gluing pages "side-by-side". Make your dictionary in two volumes, and it will be easier to use.

Use pictures from coloring books, old children's books, workbooks, etc. to make pop-up story books or song books.

POP-UP BOOKS

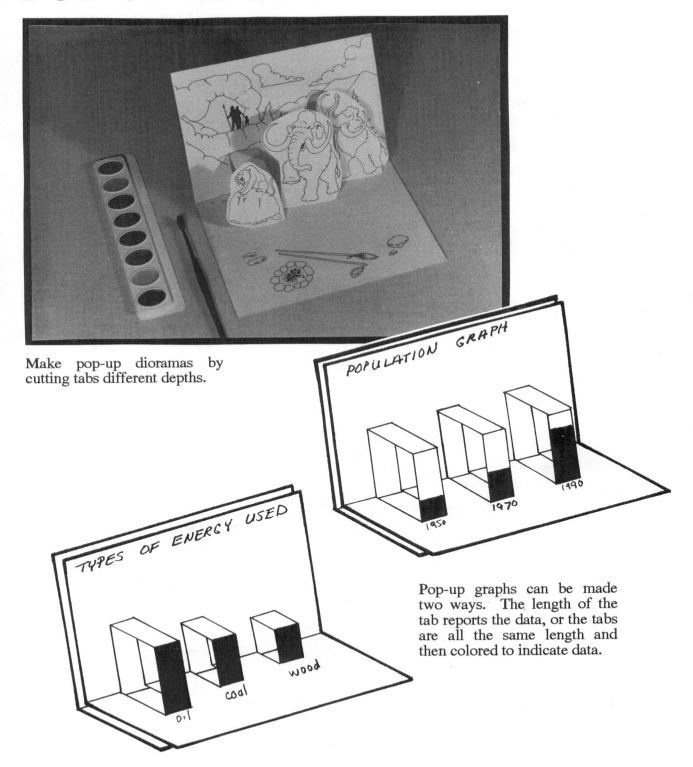

Make pop-up dioramas by cutting tabs different depths.

Pop-up graphs can be made two ways. The length of the tab reports the data, or the tabs are all the same length and then colored to indicate data.

COLORED GLUE

1. Place several drops of food coloring or cake icing dye into any size plastic bottle of glue. More drops may be added in larger bottles for darker colors.

2. Warm the bottle of glue with your hands for several minutes then shake vigorously.

3. Allow the bottle of glue to sit for 12 to 24 hours. The color will continue to spread by molecular action.

COLORED GLUE

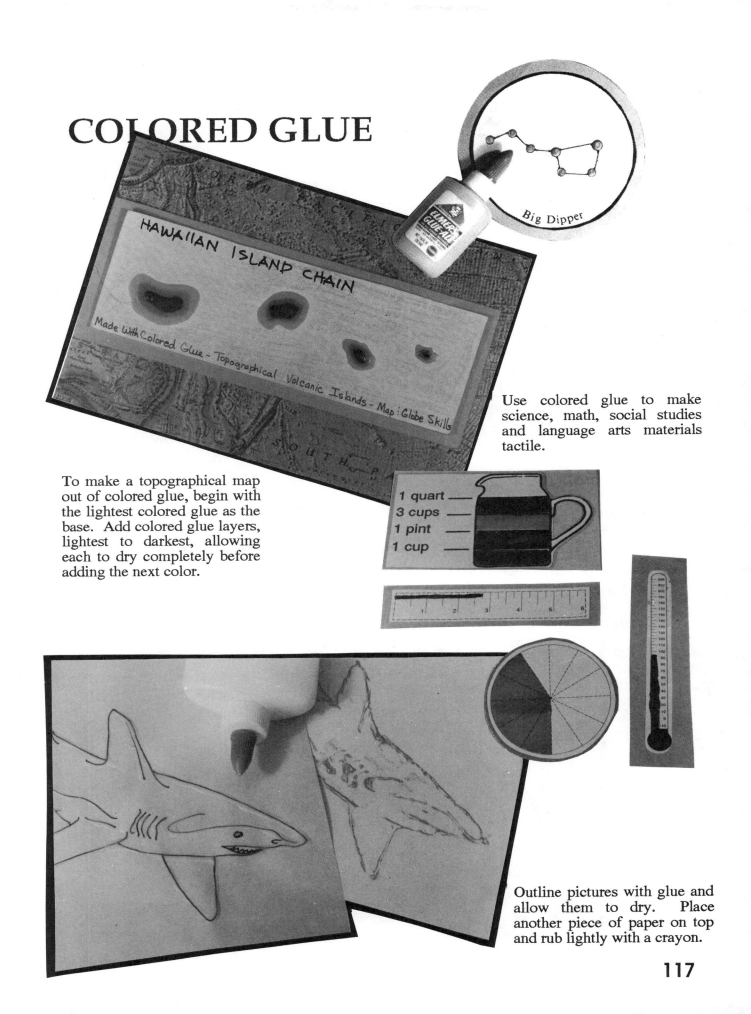

Big Dipper

HAWAIIAN ISLAND CHAIN

Made With Colored Glue - Topographical Volcanic Islands - Map : Globe Skills

Use colored glue to make science, math, social studies and language arts materials tactile.

To make a topographical map out of colored glue, begin with the lightest colored glue as the base. Add colored glue layers, lightest to darkest, allowing each to dry completely before adding the next color.

1 quart ____
3 cups ____
1 pint ____
1 cup ____

Outline pictures with glue and allow them to dry. Place another piece of paper on top and rub lightly with a crayon.

117

MACARONI MADNESS

1. Pour 1/4 cup of alcohol into a baggie. Add food coloring or cake icing dye.

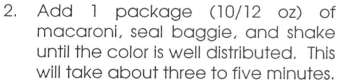

2. Add 1 package (10/12 oz) of macaroni, seal baggie, and shake until the color is well distributed. This will take about three to five minutes.

3. Pour the macaroni out of the baggie onto paper towels or newspaper. Stir occasionally and allow to dry for about fifteen minutes.

MACARONI MADNESS

Use macaroni shaped letters or numbers to label or code maps. For example, if an A is placed on a location, an A should be placed in a map key and labeled.

Glue a map onto a styrofoam board. Use tooth picks to mark specific locations. Use these small macaroni rings to form vertical bar graphs to illustrate: rainfall, topography, population, etc.

MACARONI MADNESS

Use dyed fettucini for bar graphs. One piece represents a whole. Break this piece into the fractional parts needed.

Use this bar graph with the percentage board on page 121.

Glue and label the fettucini bars as they are placed on the half book.

MACARONI MADNESS

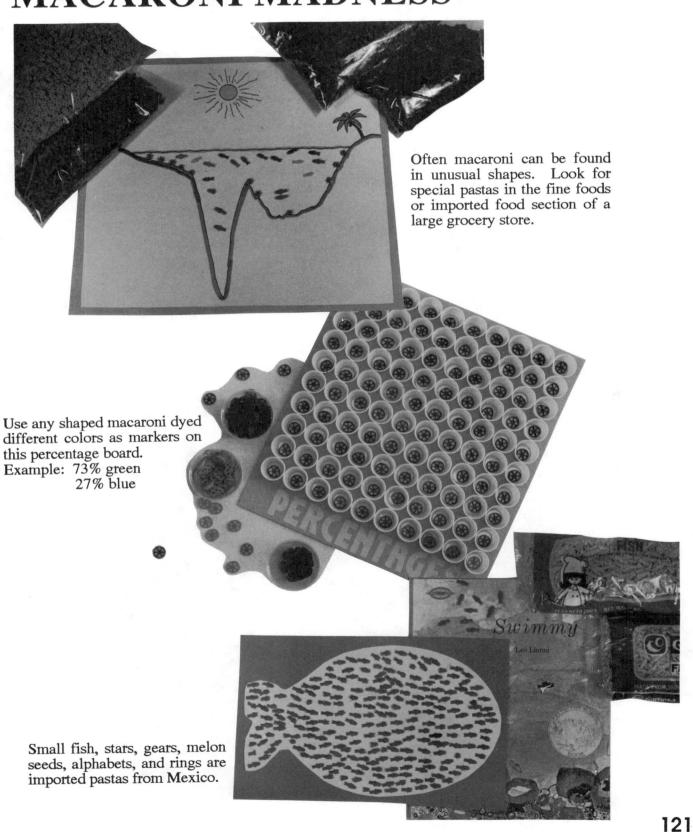

Often macaroni can be found in unusual shapes. Look for special pastas in the fine foods or imported food section of a large grocery store.

Use any shaped macaroni dyed different colors as markers on this percentage board.
Example: 73% green
         27% blue

Small fish, stars, gears, melon seeds, alphabets, and rings are imported pastas from Mexico.

COLORFUL CORNMEAL

Use one part alcohol to four parts cornmeal.

Use colored corn meal instead of sand in a homemade minute timer.

1. Pour one cup of alcohol into a baggie. Add food coloring or cake icing dye.

2. Add four cups of white cornmeal, seal the baggie, and shake until the color is well distributed.

3. Pour the cornmeal out of the baggie onto paper towels or newspaper, stir occasionally, and allow to dry for about fifteen minutes.

Glue colored cornmeal to letters, numbers, geometric shapes, or configurations of states or continents for a tactile activity.

COLORFUL CORNMEAL

Cover the bottom of a shallow box or a box lid, with brightly colored paper. Pour a contrasting color of cornmeal into the box. Finger write spelling words or practice math facts by writing in the cornmeal.

Make dioramas.

GIANT SIDEWALK CHALK

1. Place one cup of water in a DISPOSABLE container to be used for mixing.

2. Add two heaping tablespoons of dry tempera paint. Dissolve the paint in the water.

3. Add two cups plaster of Paris. DO NOT STIR. Allow the mixture to set for five minutes.

4. After five minutes, stir with a plastic spoon, or shake vigorously if in a sealed container.

5. Pour contents into four plastic or paper cups.

6. Allow to dry at room temperature, without disturbing, for 24 hours.

7. Remove the plaster from the cups and allow the chalks to continue to dry for 24 more hours before using.

GIANT SIDEWALK CHALK

Helpful Hints:

When mixing with plaster of Paris, use a ratio of 2 to 1.

Plaster of Paris can be purchased at craft stores in 4.4 pound containers, or at hardware stores in 25 pound sacks.

DO NOT rinse wet plaster from the containers into a sink. Throw away containers or wash them outside with a hose. Or, let left-over plaster dry completely inside the container, then knock it out of the container.

Pour plaster into large candy or lollipop molds to make shaped colored chalk.

Note: Do not use this chalk on a chalkboard.

TIME LINE BOOK

1. Fold two sheets of paper (8 1/2" x 11") like a hamburger.

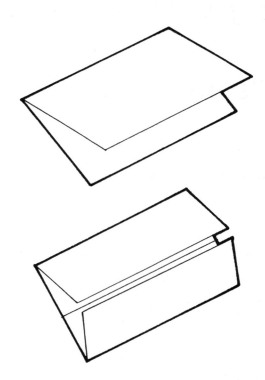

2. Fold the outer edges of both sheets toward the valley creating a shutter fold.

3. Leave the tabs hidden inside the folds.

4. Mark the edges of the single folded sides with a marker.

5. Cut both sheets in half, making each small book section the same size. Do not open.

6. Place the sections side-by-side matching the marked edges. Glue the sections together around the outer edges forming a book with pages that open and close.

TIME LINE BOOK

7. Additional book sections can be made for a longer time line.

8. Take a half sheet of construction paper and make a book cover. Construction paper is slightly larger and will leave a perfect border.

Use this book fold to make number lines.

TIME LINE BOOK

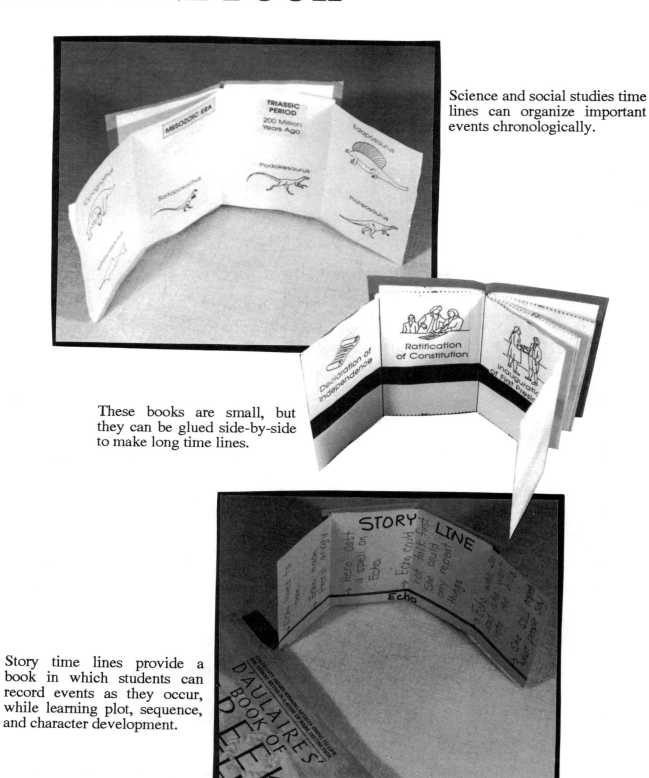

Science and social studies time lines can organize important events chronologically.

These books are small, but they can be glued side-by-side to make long time lines.

Story time lines provide a book in which students can record events as they occur, while learning plot, sequence, and character development.

NOTES

NOTES

For information on how
to book a Dinah Zike workshop
in your area, please call
(210) 698-0123
or E-mail dma@dinah.com

To receive a free catalog,
or to order other books
and materials by Dinah Zike,
please call
1-800-99DINAH (993-4624)
or
You can E-mail us at
orders@dinah.com

Visit our website at www.dinah.com

Dinah-Might Adventures, LP
P.O. Box 690328
San Antonio, Texas 78269